written by Rhonda VanCleave

Copyright © 2022 by B&H Publishing Group

All rights reserved.

Printed in the United States of America

978-1-0877-7771-9

Published by B&H Publishing Group,
Brentwood, Tennessee

Dewey Decimal Classification: 242.62
Subject Heading: DEVOTIONAL LITERATURE / PETER, APOSTLE / CHRISTIAN LIFE

1 2 3 4 5 6 7 • 26 25 24 23 22

Contents

1

Twists & Turns

*Your word is a lamp for my feet and
a light on my path.—Psalm 119:105*

Do you play board games with your family or friends? Is there sometimes an unexpected twist or turn that changes your direction or makes you rethink your next move? Sometimes life feels the same way. Twists and turns can be good. You get to do something you've always wanted, or you get chosen to be a part of an exciting new adventure. But sometimes they aren't so good. You may feel worried or sad. The new adventure could be scary.

Either way, there is good news: God is always in control! His way is always best! He can help you through every twist and turn. God gave us His Word, the Bible, to remind us that no matter how fun or scary the road might be, He is always with us and will guide us along the way. As you read the devotions in this book, you will find the story of His Son, Jesus, our Savior. The story isn't what you might expect. It's full of twists, turns, and sometimes paths that look scary and unknown. But God is always in control, and His way is always best!

Let's Play!

Can you solve the clues for this crossword puzzle?

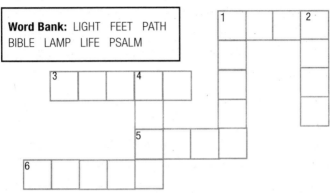

Word Bank: LIGHT   FEET   PATH   BIBLE   LAMP   LIFE   PSALM

Across
1. Provides light. Has a switch and usually sits on a table.
3. This word means "song," and is part of the reference for today's Bible verse.
5. God gave us two of these to walk on.
6. Another name for God's Word is the _____.

Down
1. The opposite of dark.
2. Another name for a walkway. It is sometimes paved with special bricks or stones.
4. God gives us _____ (the opposite of death).

Do the words you discovered sound familiar? Compare them to the key verse in the devotion (Psalm 119:105).

PRAY

Thank God for giving us His story! Ask Him to help you take time every day to read your Bible and talk to Him.

2
Read the Instructions

The instruction of the LORD is perfect,
renewing one's life.—Psalm 19:7

Tim was excited to play the game his uncle sent him for his birthday. He set up the pieces on the table. He had never played this game before, but his best friend said it was awesome. "You better read the instructions," Mom suggested. "Find out how to play, and I'll stop for a bit to play one game with you."

Tim's mom was right. Things usually go better when you know the instructions. Do you know where we can find our instructions about how to follow God? That's right! The Bible. His instructions are perfect! They help us know how to live like Jesus. They also help us see our mistakes, ask for forgiveness, and trust God to get onto His track. God's Word is amazing!

Level Up!

You read one verse from Psalm 19 in today's devotion. Can you take it to the next level? Locate Psalm 19 in your Bible and read the whole chapter. Then copy Psalm 19:14 in the space below and use it as a prayer to God.

 **PRAY**

Thank God for telling us about His love in the Bible. Ask Him to help you understand His instructions and how to follow them with your life.

3

God's Instructions Are Trustworthy

The works of his hands are truth and justice; all his instructions are trustworthy.—Psalm 111:7

Amanda looked at all the 3-D puzzle pieces tossed across the table. She started reading the instructions again, but they didn't make sense! Suddenly, Amanda remembered what her grandma used to say. "When the instructions seem complicated, don't try to understand them all at once. One at a time, Amanda. Just one at a time." Amanda decided to try that way instead of understanding all the instructions before she started. She located the first set of pieces and began putting them together. Then she did the next instruction and the next. Before she knew it, the whole puzzle was done.

Sometimes knowing what the Bible tells us can feel overwhelming. But guess what? We don't have to understand everything before we begin following Jesus with our lives. People who have followed Jesus for years still learn new things as they study God's Word. Just take the first step. God's instructions are worth our trust. He is always in control, and His way is always best!

Let's Play!

How many names of games can you find in this word search? How many have you played? Is there one you'd like to learn more about? The first step is finding the instructions!

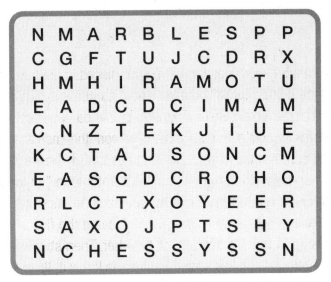

```
N M A R B L E S P P
C G F T U J C D R X
H M H I R A M O T U
E A D C D C I M A M
C N Z T E K J I U E
K C T A U S O N C M
E A S C D C R O H O
R L C T X O Y E E R
S A X O J P T S H Y
N C H E S S Y S S N
```

Word Bank: CHESS CHECKERS DOMINOES DOTS JACKS
MANCALA MARBLES MEMORY TIC TAC TOE

PRAY

Ask God to help you learn as you read your Bible. Thank Him that He welcomes all our doubts and questions!

4

Follow the Right Path

*Make your ways known to me, Lord;
teach me your paths.—Psalm 25:4*

When you play games with your friends, how far in advance do you think about your next move? Is it random? Do you have a plan for how you'll play before you start? It's almost impossible to plan out every move ahead of time, but when it comes to your life, God has a plan for you. Yes, you! He knew you before you were born. He wants you to know about Him and His love for you, and He wants you to follow Him.

A king in the Old Testament named David wrote songs praising God. They are called psalms! David was wise, and because of that, he knew he needed God's instructions to stay on God's path. He also knew that if a twist or turn came up in his life, he could trust that God would lead him. God always knows the next move! Sometimes God removed the difficulty, and sometimes God helped David go through it so that David could grow stronger. You can ask God to help you know His ways and follow His path.

Challenge Accepted!

You may have memorized Psalm 25:4 at church or VBS. If not, memorize it by writing each word on a sticky note. Each day, remove one word until you can say it without any sticky notes!

 **PRAY**

Ask God to help you know His ways. Thank Him for using the Bible to teach you about His path.

5

The Same Starting Point

Brothers and sisters, consider your calling: Not many were wise from a human perspective, not many powerful, not many of noble birth.—1 Corinthians 1:26

Jesus is the most important person who ever lived. We know Jesus is the Son of God who came to be our Savior, but when we read about other people in the Bible, like Old Testament prophets or the twelve disciples, it's easy to think they are extra important. They must have been amazing people to have their lives written about in God's Word!

But did you know they were just like you? They grew up, they did things kids do, they made some mistakes, and they did some things right. Some were seemingly insignificant at first, but God chose them to do significant things. When we focus on a person in the Bible and learn how God directed that person's path, we see how God is directing us, too. Simon Peter, one of Jesus's disciples, is someone we learn from in the Bible. As you read the rest of these devotions, you will hear about God's path for Peter's life.

Let's Play!

Play a "Draw a Person" game with a friend. You'll need a dice, paper, and pencils. Each person will take a turn rolling the dice and drawing the body part that matches the instructions below. If a person has already drawn that body part, he passes the dice to the next person without drawing anything. The first player who completes their drawing of a person is the winner!

Draw a Person

Roll a 1 – draw a head

Roll a 2 – draw the torso
        (or chest)

Roll a 3 – draw 2 arms

Roll a 4 – draw 2 legs

Roll a 5 – draw a face
        (eyes, nose, mouth)

Roll a 6 – draw hair

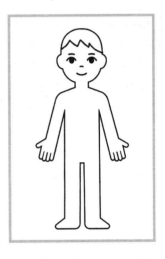

PRAY

Thank God for the opportunity to learn about Him in the Bible! Ask God to help you learn more about Jesus through Simon Peter's story.

6

Player Up: Peter

He first found his own brother Simon and told him, "We have found the Messiah" (which is translated "the Christ"), and he brought Simon to Jesus.—John 1:41

Meet Simon Peter and his brother Andrew. He was known as Simon until Jesus gave him the name Peter. Peter was a fisherman and had partners in his fishing business, including Andrew. Their lives were on track to keep doing that business, until one day, something happened that shook *everything* up.

Andrew had been following the preacher, John the Baptist, and learning from him. One day, John the Baptist pointed out Jesus to Andrew and another person who was with him. They began to follow Jesus and listen to His teaching. Andrew was amazed! He knew Jesus was the one God promised to save His people: the Messiah! The first thing he wanted to do was find his brother, Simon, and bring him to meet Jesus. So he did. When Jesus saw Simon He said, "You are Simon. You will be known as Peter." Andrew told his brother Simon about Jesus, and it changed more than Simon's name. It changed his whole life!

Level Up!

Discover more details about this Bible event. Locate John 1:35–42 in your Bible and answer these questions. Did you know that the "he" in verse 25 is John the Baptist, Jesus's cousin?

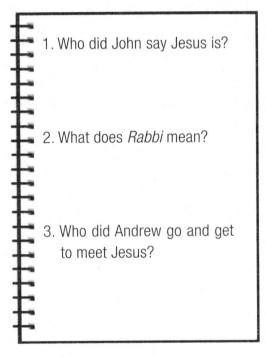

1. Who did John say Jesus is?

2. What does *Rabbi* mean?

3. Who did Andrew go and get to meet Jesus?

 **PRAY**

Ask God to help you think of someone
you can tell about Jesus.

7

Game-Changing Move

They were casting a net into the sea—for they were fishermen. "Follow me," he told them, "and I will make you fish for people."
—Matthew 4:18–19

Noah Jr., or NJ as his friends at school called him, opened his homeschool notebook. His new project was to interview three Christians and ask how God's call to follow Him changed their lives. NJ was excited to begin. He first interviewed Sara, the kids director at church; Uncle Jake, an engineer; and Mr. Baxter, his friend's dad who had his own company and helped teach a boys' discipleship group.

After NJ interviewed all three, he looked at his notes. All three people talked about how trusting Jesus as Savior was the most important decision they ever made. They all believed that their jobs were part of God's big plan for them. Mr. Baxter even said, "Before God saved me, I wasn't even able to obey God or walk on the right path. Now that God saved me, He is helping me walk in His ways!"

NJ thought about the future curiously: *I wonder how following Jesus will be step one of changing my whole life.*

Challenge Accepted!

Peter had friends who also followed Jesus. Write the names of some of your friends who also follow Jesus in the people shapes below.

 **PRAY**

If you have trusted in Jesus as your Savior, thank Him for salvation and His promise to be with you. If you haven't, ask God to help you understand what being a Christian means.

8

Joining the Team

When Simon Peter saw this, he fell at Jesus's knees and said, "Go away from me, because I'm a sinful man, Lord!"—Luke 5:8

One day, Jesus was teaching on the shore of the Sea of Galilee. The crowd kept trying to get closer to hear what He was saying. Jesus saw two boats at the edge of the water. One belonged to Simon. Jesus got in and asked Simon to put out a little way from shore. This way when Jesus spoke, everyone could hear what He said, including Simon.

After Jesus finished teaching, He told Simon to put his nets out into the deep water. Simon told Jesus, "Master, we've worked hard all night and caught nothing. But if you say so, we will." When they let the nets down, there were so many fish that the nets began to tear. They called their partners to come help. Simon Peter looked at all the fish, fell at Jesus's knees, and said, "I am a sinful man!" He didn't feel worthy to be near Jesus. Jesus told Peter not to be afraid. Peter would soon fish for people! The fishing partners then brought their boats to shore, left everything, and followed Jesus.

Level Up!

Locate Luke 5:1–11 in your Bible and read the whole story. Did you learn anything new? Draw a picture of Peter's reaction after catching the fish or write about why you think Peter reacted like he did.

 **PRAY**

Ask God to help you know what following Him means for you. Thank Him for promising to be with you even when He asks you to do scary things.

9

Immediately

Immediately they left their nets and followed him.—Mark 1:18

When your parents or teachers ask you to do something immediately, you probably don't wait around for a few more minutes, right? If you hear that word, it means to drop everything and do exactly what you were told. The Gospel of Mark uses that word to describe how a few men followed Jesus. Mark tells us that Jesus called Simon Peter, Andrew, James, and John. They would all play major roles in Jesus's ministry. Peter didn't understand then, but Jesus knew he would one day help many people came to know Jesus as Savior.

Mark says the men "immediately" left their work and families to follow Jesus. Wow! Immediately! Peter and his friends didn't know what following Jesus would be like. They just did it. Jesus wants us to trust Him the same way. What would it look like to immediately follow Jesus in your life? Have you given your life to God? Follow Him! Could it be that you are feeling a nudge to tell your friends about Jesus for the first time? Follow Him! Is there a sin in your life you need to leave behind? Follow Him! It might not be easy, but choosing to follow Jesus immediately will always be worth it.

Challenge Accepted!

Take some time to think and answer the following questions.

Peter and his friends followed Jesus immediately.
Why do you think this might have been a hard decision?

Why do you think they were willing to follow
Jesus "immediately"?

 PRAY

Ask God to make you willing
to immediately follow His commands.

10
Watch & Learn

Simon's mother-in-law was lying in bed with a fever, and they told him about her at once.—Mark 1:30

Alex volunteered to help at his aunt's vet clinic. He cleaned the cages, walked the dogs, brushed the cats, and gently held injured animals while his aunt took care of them. Alex saw firsthand what it was like to be a veterinarian, and he thought he might like to be one when he was older.

The best way to learn something is to be there, to see things happening, and to be a part of the experience. Simon Peter did that, too—but with Jesus.

Jesus had been to the synagogue in a city called Capernaum with Peter and Andrew. They left the synagogue and went to Peter and Andrew's house nearby. Peter's mother-in-law was in bed with a fever and very sick. Jesus went to her, took her by the hand, and helped her up. The fever left her right away! She even began to get food ready for the guests. Peter saw the compassion and power of Jesus firsthand. Jesus showed His compassion by dying to take the punishment for sin, and He showed His power by rising from the dead. If you believe that, you'll become a follower of Jesus like Peter, and you'll be able to point people to the compassion and power of Jesus, too!

Trivia Time!

Capernaum Facts

- Capernaum was found on the northwestern shore of the Sea of Galilee in Israel.

- Jesus lived here for a while after His ministry began (Matthew 4:13).

- Peter, Andrew, James, and John lived in Capernaum.

- Archaeologists have found a home near the Capernaum synagogue ruins that they believe to be Peter's house.

Drawing of Peter's House

- Capernaum was found along a major trade route.

- Matthew worked as a tax collector along this route.

 PRAY

Ask God to help you be compassionate and caring for others. Thank Him for Jesus's example!

11

Experience Helps

*So he touched her hand, and the fever left her.
Then she got up and began to
serve him.—Matthew 8:15*

In the previous devotion, you read from the book of Mark about Jesus healing Simon Peter's mother-in-law. Matthew told about the event in his Gospel too, but he grouped it with several stories about other times that Jesus healed people. In Matthew 8:1–17, Jesus healed a man with leprosy. He also healed the paralyzed servant of a military leader called a centurion. And Matthew wrote that Jesus healed Peter's mother-in-law by simply touching her. Sometimes Jesus wasn't even in the room. He spoke, and a person was healed.

What do you think Jesus's followers, especially His disciples, learned by observing His miracles? God made us, and He knows how we learn best. The things we see and experience help us know the power God has and how much He loves us. Think about the things you've seen or learned that help you know about God and that help you believe in Jesus.

Let's Play!

The word bank contains words found in the healing stories from Matthew 8:1–17. Do you remember what each word has to do with each miracle?

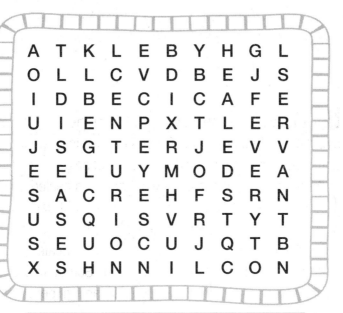

```
A  T  K  L  E  B  Y  H  G  L
O  L  L  C  V  D  B  E  J  S
I  D  B  E  C  I  C  A  F  E
U  I  E  N  P  X  T  L  E  R
J  S  G  T  E  R  J  E  V  V
E  E  L  U  Y  M  O  D  E  A
S  A  C  R  E  H  F  S  R  N
U  S  Q  I  S  V  R  T  Y  T
S  E  U  O  C  U  J  Q  T  B
X  S  H  N  N  I  L  C  O  N
```

Word Bank: CENTURION LEPROSY FEVER SERVANT
JESUS DISEASES HEALED

 **PRAY**

Ask God to help you notice the things He does for you.
Thank Him for helping you grow to know more about Him.

27

12

Amazing Power

The men were amazed and asked, "What kind of man is this? Even the winds and the sea obey him!"—Matthew 8:27

Cash and Brandon helped their dad pull the boat onto the trailer when dark clouds started rolling in. Dad quickly pulled the boat trailer up the ramp and began loading things into the truck. The wind whipped at their jackets as they gathered their things and climbed in. Just then, a flash of lightning made them jump as rain pelted against the windshield. "That was close!" Cash exclaimed. "Storms can be pretty scary."

"Yeah! And they can come up so fast!" Brandon shouted over the loud beating of the rain on the truck.

"Imagine how the disciples felt in the small wooden boats out on the Sea of Galilee," Dad said as he carefully drove the truck out of the parking lot. "And they didn't have a motor to drive them quickly to shore. Just think how amazing it was to see the waves suddenly calm and the wind stop because Jesus told them to. Jesus took care of the disciples, and He took care of us, too. What do you guys think it says about Jesus that he was able to calm the storm just by talking to it?"

Level Up!

You can read about this event in three of the Gospels. Locate each story and compare the descriptions.

In each column list:

> 1: the people in the boat
> 2: something Jesus said
> 3: something the disciples said.

Remember, Peter was one of the disciples who experienced this!

Matthew 8:23–27	Luke 8:22–25	Mark 4:35–41
1.	1.	1.
2.	2.	2.
3.	3.	3.

 PRAY

Thank God for His power over nature and ask Him to help you trust that He is in control in every situation.

13

Matthew Joins the Group

"For I didn't come to call the righteous,
but sinners."—Matthew 9:13

Matthew was a tax collector. He worked for the Roman government. In general, the Jews did not like tax collectors because they worked for Rome and took money from people. Matthew's toll booth was near Capernaum where Simon Peter was from and where Jesus was living. One day Jesus saw Matthew at the toll booth and said, "Follow Me." Matthew got up and followed Jesus.

Later, Matthew hosted a meal at his house and invited other tax collectors and people he knew. When the Pharisees (church leaders) saw Jesus going into Matthew's house, they were shocked. They asked Jesus's disciples why Jesus was eating with sinners. Jesus knew what they were thinking and told them that He came for sinners. Most people might not think Matthew was someone Jesus would want to hang around with, but Jesus is different than most people.

Challenge Accepted!

The Pharisees were church leaders who did not think Jesus should be socializing with sinners. Jesus knew the "sinners" were willing to hear the truth He had to share.

Who are some groups of people that are sometimes left out or not included?

Why do they need to be welcomed and told about Jesus?

PRAY

Ask God to help you see your sin and trust that Jesus is the only one who can save you!

14

The Twelve

He appointed twelve, whom he also named apostles, to be with him, to send them out to preach.—Mark 3:14

Nana," Keona asked on the way home from Bible study. "Sometimes my teacher says the word *apostle* and sometimes *disciple*. Are they the same thing?"

"Good question!" replied Nana. "Many people followed Jesus when He was on earth, but He chose twelve men and gave them the special task of going out and teaching others what He taught them. Jesus chose them specifically and called them apostles."

"So then who is a disciple?" Keona asked.

"Anyone who follows Jesus! The word disciple means a student or a learner. If you follow Him, you are a disciple, too. You can follow Him by reading His words in the Bible, spending time with His people at church, talking with Him through prayer, and lots of other ways. We can also look at the apostles for examples of what to do. And sometimes what not to do!"

Keona giggled. "Thanks, Nana! I can't wait to tell my friends that I am a disciple of Jesus!"

Level Up!

Can you find the names of the twelve apostles (also known as Jesus's disciples) in your Bible? Locate and read Mark 3:13–19 and fill in the list below. The first letter of each name is provided for you.

S_____ P_____ J_____

J_____ A_____

P_____ B_____

M_____ T_____

J_____ (the son of A_____) T_____

S_____ the Z_____ J_____ I_____

 **PRAY**

*Thank God that He forgives you and calls you
to be His disciple. Ask Him to help you follow
Jesus throughout your whole life.*

15

Miracles

Everyone ate and was satisfied.
—Matthew 14:20

Dad read the Bible story from Matthew 14:13–21. Eric listened carefully as Dad read about Jesus using five small bread rolls and two fish and feeding about 5,000 men, plus women and children. "How many people do you think were there?" Eric asked.

"Some people think maybe more than 15,000 since the 5,000 were just the men. No matter the actual number, it says everyone had plenty to eat, and they had twelve baskets left over." Dad explained. "Did you know this is the only miracle that is found in all four Gospel books in the New Testament? What do you think the disciples learned when they experienced such an amazing miracle?"

Eric thought for a minute, then said, "Jesus wanted people to see that He had power, and He wanted to show that He could feed them with something even better than food. He was getting ready to provide salvation! They didn't have the New Testament like we do. They were living it!"

Challenge Accepted!

When you read Scripture, pay attention to context clues to get a better idea of the story. This passage does not mention Peter, but how do you know he was probably there? Locate and read Matthew 14:15. Then use the code to complete the sentence.

When it says, "__ __ __ __ __ __ __ __ __ __ __ __ __,"
　　　　　　▼ ❋ ❋. ❋ ❋ ▲ ❋ ❋ ▢ ● ❋ ▲

it probably means all

__ __ __ __ __ __ disciples were there, including
▼ ◗ ❋ ● ❖ ❋

__ __ __ __ __ .
▢ ❋ ▼ ❋ ▢

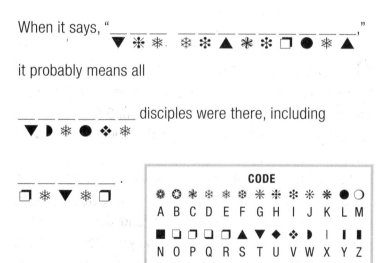

CODE												
❀	✪	✳	❋	✻	❄	✴	✵	❅	❋	✽	●	○
A	B	C	D	E	F	G	H	I	J	K	L	M
■	❑	◻	❒	◻	▲	▼	◆	❖	◗	❘	❙	❚
N	O	P	Q	R	S	T	U	V	W	X	Y	Z

PRAY

Thank God for the events you read about in your Bible that help you to know Jesus.

16

Walking on Water

*Immediately Jesus spoke to them.
"Have courage! It is I. Don't be
afraid."—Matthew 14:27*

Matthew 14:13–21 describes the time Jesus fed more than 5,000 people with five small loaves and two fish. Do you know what happened next? Another miracle! Jesus sent the apostles on ahead in a boat while He prayed. The apostles traveled some distance until the wind and waves grew so strong, they could hardly make headway. It was very early in the morning and still dark when they saw someone walking toward them on the water.

At first, they thought what they were seeing wasn't real. Then the person said, "Have courage! It is I. Don't be afraid." It was Jesus! Simon Peter asked to walk on the water to Jesus, and He said, "Come." Peter took a few steps on the water, but then he looked at the wind and the crashing waves. He became frightened and began to sink. "Help me!" Peter cried. Jesus reached out and pulled Peter up. As soon as they got into the boat, the wind stopped! The disciples all said, "Truly you are the Son of God."

Level Up!

Have you read today's story from your Bible? Locate Matthew 14:22–33 and read this story for yourself. Then, think about these questions:

The disciples had just seen the miracle of the feeding of more than 5,000 people. How did this experience add to what they had seen so far?

The Bible tells us that Jesus was with God in the beginning and everything that was made was made by Him (John 1:1–3). How did Jesus prove His power over creation?

What does this help you know about Jesus?

 **PRAY**

Thank Jesus that He truly is the Son of God. Ask Him to help you trust Him when you face scary circumstances.

17

Replay?

Jesus called his disciples and said, "I have compassion on the crowd, because they've already stayed with me three days and have nothing to eat."—Matthew 15:32

Abby liked reading the New Testament during her quiet time. As she read the end of Matthew, chapter 15, she thought, "This sounds familiar but different." She looked back in chapter 14. She was right. She had recently read about Jesus feeding more than 5,000 people, and now she had read a story about Jesus feeding more than 4,000 people.

She called her Aunt Betsy who was always excited to hear what Abby found when she read her Bible. After Abby told her aunt what she had discovered, Aunt Betsy replied, "What a great Bible detective you are! I'm glad you noticed those stories are very similar yet different. The Bible said that Jesus had compassion on both crowds, and He abundantly provided for their needs. Here's another interesting fact. The first crowd was a Jewish crowd, but the second crowd was primarily Gentile. That's anyone who isn't a Jew. Jesus did things to prove He came for everyone—Jew and Gentile alike!"

Trivia Time!

This time you can provide the trivia facts. Locate and compare the two "Feeding the Multitude" stories. Fill in the chart to compare the two stories.

	Matthew 14:13–21 (Jewish crowd)	Matthew 15:32–39 (Mostly Gentile crowd)
Number of people		
Number of loaves		
Number of fish		
Amount of leftovers		

 PRAY

Thank God for the way He provides abundantly. Thank Him that Jesus came to provide salvation to all who believe!

18

Pause the Game

He asked them, "Who do the crowds say that I am?"—Luke 9:18

Do you ever pause and pray? Sometimes during fun times, like an amazing vacation, it's great to pause to thank God for His blessings. Sometimes when things get hard, it's a good time to ask God to help you know what to do or to simply stop to remember who He is. Did you know that Jesus often stopped what He was doing to pray? Sometimes He prayed alone, and sometimes He prayed with His disciples.

After Luke described the feeding of the 5,000 in his Gospel, he recorded a time when Jesus was praying in private with His disciples. Jesus asked, "Who do the crowds say I am?" The disciples said that some people thought Jesus was John the Baptist, or Elijah, or another one of the ancient prophets. Then Jesus asked, "But who do you say that I am?"

Simon Peter answered quickly, "You are God's Messiah." Jesus wanted to remind the disciples that He is who God sent to save His people, but He warned them not to tell anyone yet. Things would soon get hard for the disciples, and they needed to pause and remember Him.

Challenge Accepted!

You've begun to learn about the things Peter experienced while he followed Jesus. What has Peter done that sounds like something you would do?

What have you learned about Jesus as you've studied the Scriptures in this devotional?

What are some questions you still have about things you've read in the Bible?

 **PRAY**

Thank God for sending Jesus as the Messiah and saving the world through His death and resurrection!

19

Knowing Who Jesus Is

"But you," he asked them, "Who do you say that I am?"—Mark 8:29

Matthew and Mark also wrote about the time when Jesus asked His disciples who people thought He was. Matthew and Mark included that Jesus and the disciples were on the way to Caesarea Philippi. This was a town named to honor Caesar Augustus. The disciples didn't fully understand that Jesus came to be the Savior. They were beginning to understand that Jesus was the Messiah, but they still thought it would involve a kingdom on earth. They thought Jesus would someday overthrow Rome and take political control. Jesus was trying to help them understand. In fact, Jesus asked the question as they were traveling near a city that was dedicated to the powers of Rome.

Simon Peter and the rest of the disciples had a hard time understanding all the things Jesus told them, but they were beginning to. Jesus had patience and continued to teach them. Jesus has patience with us, too. He wants us to follow Him, and He is patient with us when we still have a lot to learn.

Trivia Time!

Caesarea Philippi

- It is located about 25 miles north of the Sea of Galilee.
- It is near Mount Hermon.
- Herod the Great built a temple there to honor Caesar Augustus.
- Herod gave the city to his son Philip.

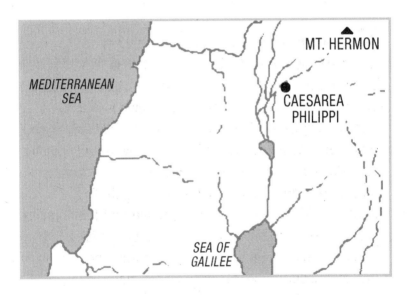

 **PRAY**

Thank God for His patience with you and for helping you learn more about Jesus and why He came.

20

Know the Truth

*Jesus responded, "Blessed are you,
Simon son of Jonah, because flesh and
blood did not reveal this to you, but my
Father in heaven."—Matthew 16:17*

Andre enjoyed making notes in his journal as he compared similar events in the Bible. He read Matthew 16:13–20 and thought about the same event described in Mark and Luke. When Simon Peter answered that Jesus is the Messiah, Jesus said, "Blessed are you, Simon, son of Jonah, because flesh and blood did not reveal this to you, but my Father in heaven." *What!?* Andre thought. Andre showed the verse to his dad and asked what it meant.

Dad took Andre's Bible and pointed to the words as he explained, "Flesh and blood means people. Jesus meant that Peter was beginning to understand some very important truths, not because people told him, but because God helped him understand. God helps us understand, too."

"If God helps people understand the Bible, why didn't I understand what that verse meant?" Andre asked.

"Well, sometimes God helps us understand by giving us people to explain it. So, in a way, God was helping you through my answer. Our source of truth is still God, just like He was for Peter."

Let's Play!

Can you unscramble some key words from today's Bible study?

SJSUE

_____

IPCISSDLE

_____

REEPT

_____

HAEMSIS

_____

HATREF NI EEANVH

_____

 **PRAY**

*Ask God to help you understand truth
as you study your Bible.*

45

21

Stay or Go?

Simon Peter answered, "Lord, to whom will we go? You have the words of eternal life."—John 6:68

Natalie was so excited to be at church camp. Susan, her Bible study leader, made everything so interesting. One day Natalie said, "I wish I could have been one of Jesus's disciples. It must have been amazing to hear Jesus teach every day and to spend time with Him."

Susan nodded in agreement. "I know what you mean. But did you know that some of the people who followed Jesus had a hard time accepting what Jesus taught? Some of them even stopped following Him and went back to their regular lives. Jesus asked His twelve chosen disciples if any of them wanted to leave Him, too. Simon Peter was the one who said, 'Lord, to whom will we go? You have the words of eternal life.'"

"Really?" Natalie exclaimed. "It's sad that people were right there with Jesus and turned away. I agree with Peter! I want to always follow Jesus."

Susan reminded Natalie, "That's right, but remember, Jesus teaches some challenging things. We should pray and ask Him to give us the courage and commitment to obey Him even if it's difficult."

Let's Play!

Peter promised to keep following Jesus. Can you help Peter get through the maze to Jesus?

Peter

JESUS

PRAY

Ask God to help you accept the truth in His Word and pray He will help you always follow Jesus.

22

Transfigured!

"This is my beloved Son, with whom I am well-pleased. Listen to him!"—Matthew 17:5

Tristan slowly sounded out the word as he read his Bible passage for the day. "Trans-fig-u-ra-tion. Mom, did I say that word right? What does it mean?"

"You did! Good job." Mom encouraged Tristan. "Transfiguration is when someone's appearance suddenly changes. You are reading about Jesus taking Simon Peter, James, and John up on a tall mountain by themselves. While they were there He was *transfigured*. His face shone like the sun, and His clothes became as white as light! A bright cloud suddenly covered them and they heard God's voice in the cloud. God said that Jesus was His beloved Son, and He was pleased with Him."

"Wow!" exclaimed Tristan. "That must have been scary and exciting for Peter, James, and John!"

"It was," Mom agreed. "They fell on their faces in fear. But Jesus helped them up and told them not to be afraid. When we see Jesus for who He is, we never have to be afraid again."

Level Up!

Locate Matthew 17:1–9 and read about the transfiguration in your Bible.

Why do you think Peter, James, and John were afraid?

Why do you think Jesus wanted them to experience His transfiguration?

 **PRAY**

*Thank God for the many things in the Bible
that help you see who Jesus is.*

23

Go Fish

"But, so we won't offend them, go to the sea, cast in a fishhook, and take the first fish that you catch."—Matthew 17:27

One day Jesus and the disciples went to Capernaum. People were expected to pay a temple tax of two drachma (about the cost of two sheep) per adult man to support the temple. The ones who collected the tax asked Simon Peter if Jesus paid the temple tax. When Peter asked Jesus about it. Jesus explained that they would pay the tax so they didn't offend those at the temple. He told Peter to go over to the Sea of Galilee and throw in a hook.

Peter was to take the first fish he caught and look in its mouth. Peter did what he was told and, sure enough, there was a coin in the fish's mouth that was enough to pay the temple tax for Jesus and Peter. Jesus didn't come to keep His people from having to pay taxes. He asks us to obey the laws set around us, but He doesn't leave us alone. He always provides for His people!

Let's Play!

Solve the code to find the missing letters. Can you use these sentences to tell someone the story you read today?

Peter usually used ___ ___ ___ ___ to catch fish.

One day Jesus told Peter to use a ___ ___ ___ ___

and keep the ___ ___ ___ ___ ___ fish he caught.

A ___ ___ ___ ___ was in the fish's mouth.

It was enough to cover the tax for ___ ___ ___ ___ ___

and ___ ___ ___ ___ ___ .

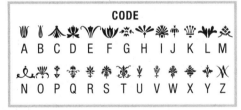

CODE

A	B	C	D	E	F	G	H	I	J	K	L	M

N	O	P	Q	R	S	T	U	V	W	X	Y	Z

PRAY

Thank God that He always provides for His people, even in unexpected ways!

24

Alive to Play Again

"Don't be afraid. Only believe."—**Mark 5:36**

Simon Peter and the other disciples were often there when Jesus performed miracles. One day, a temple official named Jairus came to Jesus because his young daughter was very sick and about to die. Jesus and those with Him began to walk to Jairus's house. But Jesus didn't rush; in fact, He even made time to heal another woman along the way! Before they could get there, some of the people of Jairus's house came to them and told them the little girl had died. Jesus looked at Jairus and said, "Don't be afraid. Only believe."

Many people were gathered at the house. Jesus told everyone to leave except His three disciples and the girl's parents. They went into her room, and Jesus took her by the hand. "Little girl, get up." Immediately, she got up and went to her parents. Jesus gave that little girl new life, and He came to give us new life! He gives us new spiritual life when we believe in Him, and one day, when He comes back, all of His followers will be raised from the dead and given a new physical life as well.

Challenge Accepted!

Gospel writers wrote the events down so people would remember what happened. Keep a journal of the times you know God has provided for you or protected you. Reading about those times later can help you remember how God loves you and is with you.

 **PRAY**

Thank Jesus that He is always in control,
even on the scariest days! Ask Him to help
you trust Him when you are worried.

25

Jesus Knows

*"Who touched me?" Jesus
asked.—Luke 8:45*

Olivia listened carefully as Ashley, her small group leader, talked about Jairus, the temple official who asked Jesus to come heal his young daughter. "But on the way to Jairus's house, something else amazing happened!" Ashley said with excitement. "A woman was in the tight crowd who had been suffering with a bleeding issue for twelve years. She spent all she had on doctors, but nothing helped. So, she followed behind Jesus until she was close enough to touch the bottom of His robe. She believed touching Jesus would be enough to heal her. She trusted in His power, and instantly, she was healed! Jesus stopped and said, 'Who touched me?'"

"How did He know it was her?" Olivia asked.

Ashley replied, "That's exactly what Simon Peter asked. Jesus knew because He had felt the healing power go out of Him. The woman was afraid at first, but Jesus called her 'daughter' and told her that her faith had saved her, and she was healed."

Trivia Time!

Medicine in New Testament Times

Not much is recorded about medicine during the time of Jesus, but here are a few things we can learn from Scripture.

 The woman in today's story had gone to many doctors looking for healing.

 Luke (the writer of the Gospel of Luke) was a physician who traveled with Paul.

 In the parable of the good Samaritan, Jesus told about the Samaritan using oil and bandages to care for the wounded man.

 PRAY

Thank God for Jesus's power to do amazing things.
Ask Him to help you trust Jesus always.

26

Forgiveness Math

"Lord, how many times must I forgive my brother or sister who sins against me?"
—Matthew 18:21

Sam, you need to forgive your brother. He didn't mean to bump the table while you were doing your homework, and he has apologized," Mom said sternly.

"I have to forgive him every day. That's seven days a week! And 365 days a year!!" Sam said, more agitated with each number he spouted off. But Mom wasn't upset. She smiled as if she understood Sam's frustration.

"Did you know Simon Peter asked Jesus a similar question? Let's look it up in Matthew 18." They read verses 21–22. Sam did some math in his mind and asked, "So, since 70 x 7 equals 490, I only have to forgive him for a little more than a year!"

Mom laughed. "Jesus didn't mean to count them. He meant to stop counting. Jesus taught His followers to be generous with their forgiveness because He has been generous with His forgiveness. If Jesus forgives us for all the ways we wrong Him, we can forgive others, too."

Let's Play!

Read Matthew 18:21–22. Can you find some of the words from the Scripture verses in the word search?

```
U Y Y N G S J A T K
F N P V B E F M T N
S S N N R V O K I J
H I K Y O E R J M M
M D S Y T N G E E V
P S K T H T I S S S
E M M F E Y V U P E
T X P P R R E S E V
E U O M Z C A D O E
R T X Y U P B X N N
```

Word Bank: BROTHER FORGIVE SEVENTY SISTER
SEVEN JESUS PETER TIMES

 **PRAY**

*Thank God for forgiving you even more than
490 times, and ask God to help you forgive
the way Jesus taught His disciples to.*

27

Being Humble

*"Whoever humbles himself like this child—
this one is the greatest in the kingdom
of heaven."—Matthew 18:4*

Mom!" Gabriela exclaimed. "Sofia is ruining my homework! She needs to keep her crayon marks on her paper. Mine is too important"

Mom carefully moved Sofia's chair farther down the kitchen table. She placed Sofia's coloring book and crayons where Sofia could reach them. "Your homework is important, Gabriela," Mom said. "But Sofia doesn't understand the difference, and her coloring is important to her, too."

"I sah-ree," Sofia said in a tiny voice.

"Jesus's disciples were impatient with the little children, too," Mom added. "But Jesus told the disciples that they needed to be humble like little children if they wanted to be truly great in the kingdom of heaven. I know you want to do a good job on your homework, but kindness to your sister is also important."

Let's Play!

Great to Small

How many smaller words can you make using the letters in this phrase?

KINGDOM OF HEAVEN

PRAY

Ask God to help you think of others first.

28

Something to Think About

*Then his disciples asked him, "What does
this parable mean?"—Luke 8:9*

On the way to Bible study, Ricky suddenly remembered an assignment he had for that night. "Dad!" Ricky called from the backseat. "I was supposed to find out what a parable is, and I forgot. Do you know what that means?"

Dad thought a minute, then replied, "It's a story that makes people think deeply about something complicated. Jesus told parables to teach people things about His kingdom. He showed them that our hearts and our world is nothing like His. And even though He knew that the parables would confuse some, He also knew they would help others."

"Do you know any parables?" Ricky asked.

"I do." Dad replied. "You will probably study one of Jesus's parables tonight based on your assignment. When we get home, I'll tell you one of my favorites. Sometimes we have to really think about them to understand, but the Holy Spirit helps us, too. Let's pray and ask God to help you understand the parable you hear tonight."

"Okay, but don't close your eyes while you drive!" Ricky said. "I don't think Mom would like that."

Trivia Time!

Circle all the facts you already knew!

Parables are stories Jesus told to help people understand the kingdom of God.

Some parables can be found in only one Gospel book. Some are found in two or three.

Matthew and Luke record the most parables (more than thirty each).

A few parables for you to check out:

The parable about the wise and foolish builders can be found in Matthew 7:24–27 and Luke 6:47–49.

Three parables about how heaven rejoices when someone trusts in Jesus (Luke 15:4–32).

 **PRAY**

Thank God for helping you understand His Word.
Ask Him to help you as you learn more about Him.

29

Picture a Parable

"This is the meaning of the parable: The seed is the word of God."—Luke 8:11

Jesus told one parable about four kinds of soil. When a farmer scattered the seeds, they grew differently based on the soil where they landed. Jesus's disciples asked what the parable meant.

Jesus explained that the seed represented God's Word, and the soils represented different ways people respond. The seeds that fell on the path or hard soil are like people who never believe the truth of God's Word. The seeds that fell on the rocky soil are like people who listen just a little, but the truth doesn't take root in their hearts. They never fully believe either. The seeds that fell among thorny weeds are like people who hear the Word of God and never grow because they are more concerned with other things. Finally, the seeds that fell on the good ground were like people who hear the Word of God and truly believe. They "bear fruit," which means they do things that honor and obey God. Which soil is like your heart?

Challenge Accepted!

Draw a picture of the four types of soil Jesus told about in His parable. Write a short reminder of what type of person each soil represented.

HARD SOIL	ROCKY SOIL

THORNY SOIL	GOOD SOIL

 PRAY

Ask God to help you be like the good soil.
Pray He will make His Word take root in your
heart so you can grow and follow Him.

30

Ponder Another Parable

But wanting to justify himself, he asked Jesus,
"And who is my neighbor?"—Luke 10:29

Grandpa walked into the room and saw Emma busy at work, writing in her journal. She had her Bible and a list on the table near her. "What are you up to this morning?" Grandpa asked.

"We have been talking about Jesus's parables in Bible study," Emma replied. "I decided to look up as many as I can and list them in my journal."

"That's a great plan, Emma," Grandpa encouraged her. "Have you read about the good Samaritan? That is one of my favorites."

"I have, but will you remind me?" Emma asked.

Grandpa smiled. "A law expert asked Jesus the question, 'Who is my neighbor?' Jesus told a parable about a man who was robbed and hurt. People who you'd expect to help him walked past. They never even stopped to help him! But then, a man you would never expect to help stopped and took care of the hurting man. Jesus was reminding the law expert that we should be kind to everyone, no matter who they are."

Level Up!

Locate Luke 10:25–37 and read the parable of the good Samaritan. What if this happened today? Who might Jesus have talked about in His parable?

Who are some people you know who need help?

Who are some people you would expect to be helpers? What about those who would not be helpers?

What was Jesus trying to help the people understand?

 **PRAY**

Ask God to help you treat everyone with kindness even when it's not the popular thing to do.

31

Little Children

"Let the little children come to me."—Mark 10:14

Jesus often changed the way Simon Peter and the other disciples thought about things. They were learning that Jesus was the Messiah, the person God promised to send to save His people. They saw Him perform miracles and do amazing things. One day, some parents were bringing their little children to Jesus so He could bless them. The disciples scolded the parents. At that time in history, people thought children were an annoyance.

When Jesus saw the disciples, He was upset with them. Jesus told the disciples to let the little children come to Him. Jesus explained to His disciples that it takes simple trust, the kind small children have, to follow Him. Jesus then turned to the children, welcomed them, and blessed them. Jesus has time for children. He cares about people the world thinks are unimportant or annoying. He welcomes all of us who come to believe and trust in Him.

Challenge Accepted!

Imagine you were one of the children who were welcomed by Jesus. You were able to see Him and hear Him bless you. How would you feel?

Remember, even though you can't see Him physically, but Jesus sees you and hears you. He loves you and welcomes you.

 **PRAY**

Thank God that you don't have to be a grown-up to trust Jesus. Praise Him that Jesus loves you and invites you to come to Him.

32

Who's the Greatest?

"For even the Son of Man did not come to be served, but to serve, and to give his life as a ransom for many."—Mark 10:45

Zion tossed his soccer ball into the back of the minivan. "Joe thinks he's so special because his dad's the coach," Zion grumbled. "He acts like he's the most important player on the team. We all work hard!"

"I know you do," Mom agreed as she started the van. "But I've watched your coach, and he's always fair with all the players. I think it bothers him that his son acts like that, but he doesn't give him special treatment. Did you know even Jesus had a problem with His 'team'? A couple of His disciples, James and John, asked for the best places in Jesus's kingdom."

"Really?" Zion asked in surprise. "The disciples had ego problems?"

"Some of them did," Mom replied. "But Jesus told them that whoever wants to be great must first be willing to be a servant to others. In fact, Jesus said that He came to serve, not to be served, and to sacrifice His life for sinful people like you and me who don't deserve it."

Let's Play!

Turn each squiggle line into a drawing of something you can use to serve others. It might be a flower to take to someone who is sad or a bucket of water you could use to help someone wash a car. What are your great ideas?

 PRAY

Ask God to humble you when you think you're better than someone else. Thank Him for teaching you how to treat others with kindness.

33

Just Talking

"But when you pray, go into your private room, shut your door, and pray to your Father who is in secret. And your Father who sees in secret will reward you."—Matthew 6:6

Kathryn was excited when all the grandkids got to spend the night with Nana and Grandpa. Grandpa gathered everyone together for prayer time before bed. Kathryn listened to Grandpa pray. He prayed to God just like he talked to a friend. One day, Kathryn asked Grandpa, "How do you know how to pray?"

"Prayer is talking to God like you talk to people you know," Grandpa explained. "God knows what we are thinking. So, we can speak honestly with Him. There are different times that we pray. Sometimes it is with a lot of people, and sometimes it's only Nana and me. Most of the time I pray when it's just God and me. I can pray in my thoughts or out loud. It doesn't matter, God hears either way. I feel closer to God when we're just talking."

Let's Play!

Jesus taught His disciples to pray. You can find one example in Matthew 6:9–13. Can you find some of the words from this model prayer in the word search?

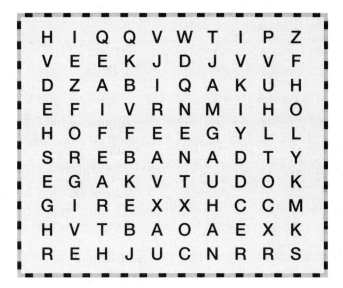

H	I	Q	Q	V	W	T	I	P	Z
V	E	E	K	J	D	J	V	V	F
D	Z	A	B	I	Q	A	K	U	H
E	F	I	V	R	N	M	I	H	O
H	O	F	F	E	E	G	Y	L	L
S	R	E	B	A	N	A	D	T	Y
E	G	A	K	V	T	U	D	O	K
G	I	R	E	X	X	H	C	C	M
H	V	T	B	A	O	A	E	X	K
R	E	H	J	U	C	N	R	R	S

Word Bank: KINGDOM   FORGIVE   FATHER   HEAVEN
EARTH   DAILY   BREAD   HOLY

PRAY

*Talk to God about what's happening
to you today. Maybe it's an ordinary day.
Tell Him your favorite thing about today.*

34

Teach Us to Pray

"Lord, teach us to pray."—Luke 11:1

Do you have a hard time concentrating when you pray? Do your thoughts wander? Then you are like a lot of people. A guide for personal prayer time can really help. Matthew and Luke both include a model prayer Jesus shared with His disciples. Some people call this "The Lord's Prayer," and some say it from memory as part of their focused prayer time. Others prefer to use it to explain the different ways to pray.

Either way, Jesus's model helps us remember things we should pray about. His model included praise to God for who He is. It modeled submission or saying God's will is more important than ours. It modeled petition or requesting something from God. It also modeled forgiveness. How can you pray with praise, submission, petition, and forgiveness? Try to pray like this today when you talk to God!

Level Up!

Some people use the word "ACTS" to guide their prayer time. Read what each letter stands for and spend some time praying based on each prayer prompt.

A – *Adoration:* Prayers that praise God for who He is.

C – *Confession:* Confessing our sins to God and asking for forgiveness restores our relationship with God.

T – *Thanksgiving:* Thank God for the many blessings He has given and the many ways He provides.

S – *Supplication:* Supplication means requesting or asking God for help with specific needs. You can pray for yourself and others.

 PRAY

Praise God for His goodness!
Thank God for teaching us how to pray!

35
Why Worry?

"Therefore I tell you, don't worry about your life, what you will eat; or about the body, what you will wear."—Luke 12:22

Diego watched the bird feeder through the window. He didn't like being sick, but he didn't feel like going outside either. Instead, he enjoyed watching the many different birds who came to eat each day. He could identify each bird that came to the feeders. When he saw a new one, he wrote it down in his bird book. Sometimes he drew sketches of the birds in his book. Diego thought about how God took care of even the smallest bird. He opened his Bible to a passage he was trying to memorize, Luke 12:22–26.

It said that God takes care of the ravens. Diego's favorite part of the verse was, "Aren't you worth much more than the birds?" It was a reminder that worrying doesn't fix anything, so why worry? God cared enough about the birds at the feeder to take care of them, and Diego trusted that God cared even more about him.

Challenge Accepted!

Drawing Challenge

1. Place your pencil on the paper.
2. Look at an object carefully, then close your eyes.
3. Try to draw it without picking up your pencil.
4. Open your eyes and see how you did!

Was it hard to draw without looking? We can be thankful God sees everything, all the time, even when we don't. We can trust God.

PRAY

Tell God what worries you and ask Him to help you trust Him.

36
Following the Rules

"The Son of Man is Lord even of the Sabbath."—Mark 2:28

During Jesus's time, it was unusual to have a copy of the Scriptures at home. The scrolls were usually at the synagogue, and people went there to hear them read aloud. The Pharisees and other religious leaders studied the Scriptures and taught the people. However, over the years, they added rules to the Scriptures, probably to help the people know how to obey God's law. However, over the years, they added rules to the Scriptures. They were probably trying to help people obey God's laws, but the problem was, they started acting like their rules were just as important as God's.

One Sabbath the disciples broke one of the new rules by picking grain on the Sabbath, and the Pharisees became angry. But Jesus reminded them that the "Son of Man" (a name He used for Himself) is Lord of the Sabbath, or in other words, Jesus created and owns all God's rules. He knows them inside and out, and He would know if the disciples were disobeying God. God's rules are more important than our own, and His rules are for our benefit.

Let's Play!

Do you remember the words in this crossword from today's devotion?

Across

2. A special day to rest and worship
4. Jesus is _____ of the Sabbath.
5. The disciples picked some _____ to eat.

Down

1. Religious leaders that added rules for people to obey.
3. The disciples had not eaten and they were _____.

Word Bank: PHARISEES GRAIN LORD HUNGRY SABBATH

PRAY

Thank God for His rules that are in the Bible to protect us and help us.

37

Raising Lazarus

*"I am the resurrection and the life.
The one who believes in me, even
if he dies, will live."—John 11:25*

Jesus had friends who lived in the towns where they traveled. In the town of Bethany, Jesus sometimes visited siblings named Martha, Mary, and Lazarus. One day, Lazarus became very sick, and his sisters sent for Jesus. But Jesus didn't come right away. He knew God had something important for His followers to learn. When Jesus did arrive in Bethany, Lazarus had been dead for four days. Martha was sad because she believed Jesus could have healed her brother if He had been there, but Jesus explained that He is the resurrection and the life. Martha thought she knew what Jesus meant.

Ultimately, Lazarus would live again with God in heaven, but she wanted Jesus to have kept him alive on earth. Jesus went to the tomb and prayed aloud to the Father so those who heard would know He came from God. Then Jesus called Lazarus's name, and he walked out of the tomb! Martha knew that day that Jesus has power over life in heaven and life on earth. He can make anyone live!

Level Up!

Find John 11:1–45 and read about the events that happened when Lazarus was sick and died.

What questions did the disciples ask?

What did Jesus raising Lazarus from the dead help the people know about God's power?

Do you think the disciples thought about this event after Jesus was crucified?

 PRAY

Tell Jesus about your fears of death. Thank Him that He is the resurrection and the life!

38

God's Details

*"Go and make preparations for us to
eat the Passover."—Luke 22:8*

Miss Maria asked Carly to help her prepare for the communion service on Sunday. "Some people call this communion and some call it the Lord's Supper." Carly said. "Which is it?"

"Either way is okay," Miss Maria explained. "When Jesus and His followers first had this meal, they were celebrating Passover to remember how God rescued the Israelites from slavery in Egypt. But He was about to rescue God's people from a different kind of slavery: the slavery to sin. All people are born into sin, and we all deserve punishment for our sins. But when Jesus gave His body and blood—His life—He freed us from that punishment.

"So both of these are reminders?" Carly asked.

"Exactly," Miss Maria agreed. "God wants us to remember the details of the things He has done for us."

Trivia Time!

Passover Facts

- God told the Israelites to celebrate Passover every year to remember how He rescued them from slavery in Egypt.

- Jesus always celebrated Passover when He lived on earth.

- Jewish people today still celebrate Passover.

- Passover is celebrated for seven days (or eight in some places).

- Six symbolic foods are traditionally part of the Passover meal: a boiled egg, haroset (a sweet mix of fruits, nuts, and honey), karpas (a green vegetable like parsley), bitter herbs (often horseradish), hazeret (lettuce), and a shank bone from a lamb.

 **PRAY**

Thank Jesus for loving you enough to take the punishment for your sins. Ask Him to help you remember all the ways He has helped you.

39
Understanding Takes Time

His disciples did not understand these things at first. However, when Jesus was glorified, then they remembered.—John 12:16

Amari talked to his mom after the family got home from small group Bible study. "I don't want to go back to Bible study," he groaned.

"Why?" his mom asked softly. She could tell Amari was upset. "What happened?"

"Nothing happened," Amari replied. "I just don't understand all the things we read in the Bible. Some of it makes sense, but I'm not even sure what questions to ask about other parts. Our teacher does a good job, but everyone else knows more than me."

"I understand," Mom nodded in agreement. "Did you know that Jesus's own disciples didn't always understand the things Jesus told them at first? They didn't even understand after He told them multiple times!"

"Really?" Amari asked, surprised.

"But when the time was right, they remembered, and they understood." Mom explained. "God will help you know what you need to know. Our responsibility is to keep reading His Word and studying."

Challenge Accepted!

What are some things you don't understand that you've read about in the Bible? Write them down here and, as you learn more, add the things you discover.

PRAY

Ask God to help you keep reading His Word, even when you don't understand. He will encourage you to learn.

40

You Serve

He came to Simon Peter, who asked him, "Lord, are you going to wash my feet?"—John 13:6

Jesus knew it was His last meal with His disciples before He would be arrested and crucified. But the disciples did not know. Before the meal, Jesus washed the disciples' feet. When Jesus got to Simon Peter, he couldn't believe that Jesus would want to touch his dusty feet. When Peter asked if Jesus was about to wash his feet, Jesus explained that it was important. So, Peter said, "Lord, not only my feet, but my hands and my head." It was clear that Peter was confused.

Jesus was teaching them something important. He was their teacher, but He was willing to humble Himself to serve them. They should be willing to do the same for each other—to do dirty jobs because they loved each other. Peter had been with Jesus for a long time, but he was still learning.

Level Up!

Locate this story in your Bible and read about what happened (John 13:1–11).

How do you think you would have reacted if Jesus bent down to wash your feet?

PRAY

Thank God that Jesus came to serve us and save us, and ask Him to help you serve others like Jesus did.

41

Follow the Leader

"For I have given you an example,
that you also should do just as I
have done for you."—John 13:15

Jesus finished washing the disciples' feet. He even washed the feet of Judas, who He knew would soon betray Him. He sat back down at the table and talked to the disciples about why He had just given them that example. Jesus explained that no one is greater than anyone else, no matter what their job or rank might be. In fact, even if they felt they had more power than someone else, they should still be willing to serve.

When Jesus said, "You also should do just as I have done for you," He was telling them to be willing to serve other people in whatever way necessary to help them know about Him. Jesus was preparing them for His death, which He knew would be the next day. Jesus's death was the ultimate way He came to serve—by taking the punishment we deserve for our sin. The Bible even calls Jesus "the Suffering Servant." He was teaching them and showing them examples of how they would continue to be His disciples, even when He wasn't with them anymore.

Challenge Accepted!

Think about these questions:

> Where will you have opportunities to serve others this week?
>
>
> Is it easy or difficult to serve others?
>
>
> Is it easy or difficult to allow others to serve you?

 PRAY

Ask God to help you discover ways to serve others even when you don't feel like it.

42

Jesus Always Knows

Simon Peter motioned to [John] to find out who it was [Jesus] was talking about.
—John 13:24

After Jesus washed His disciples' feet and talked with them about serving others, He had a very strange thing to tell them. Jesus knew that one of the disciples would betray Him. He even knew which one! When Jesus said, "One of you will betray me," most of the disciples were shocked and started looking at one another.

Simon Peter motioned to John to find out who Jesus was talking about. When John asked Jesus, Jesus simply said that it was the one He had given a piece of bread to that had been dipped in the oil. That could have been anyone at the table. But Judas knew he was the one, and he got up to leave. Jesus even said, "What you're doing, do quickly."

The disciples still had no clue what was about to happen. Judas took care of their money. They thought Jesus was sending Judas to buy the things they still needed for the festival or to give something to the poor. It wasn't time for the disciples to know, but Jesus knew.

Let's Play!

Find these words from the story in today's word search.

```
P O O R Q J J P Z L
Y W W C J E U G R T
F P A N O S D M O A
P E E F H U A T D B
B C S T N S S M B L
I E S T E B Q O R E
H J T Q I R C N E S
M V B R F V E E A A
U E L Z A W A Y D Q
H G R V W Y X L S F
```

Word Bank: FESTIVAL PETER JUDAS TABLE JESUS
BETRAY POOR BREAD MONEY JOHN

 **PRAY**

*Thank God that He knows everything and
that you can trust Him, even when you
don't know what the future holds.*

43

Jesus Knows Our Thoughts

"Truly I tell you, a rooster will not crow until you have denied me three times."
—John 13:38

Liam was helping his big sister work in their yard, but he kept thinking about last Sunday's Bible lesson. "I can't stop thinking about the Last Supper," Liam told his big sister, Callie. "He was eating with them, and He knew the whole time Judas was going to betray Him!"

Callie added, "Jesus also knew Simon Peter would deny that he even knew Jesus. Jesus told Peter it would happen before the rooster crowed."

"But how could He still love someone who was about to deny Him to everyone?" Liam wondered. He was confused, but Callie placed her arm around his shoulder.

"He knew that Peter would deny Him, but He loved Peter anyway. That's how amazing the love of Jesus is: even when we fail Him, He doesn't stop loving us. Speaking of failure—you better stop avoiding this yard work!" Liam giggled, and the two got back to work.

Let's Play!

Use the code to solve the missing words. Why are these words important to today's devotional?

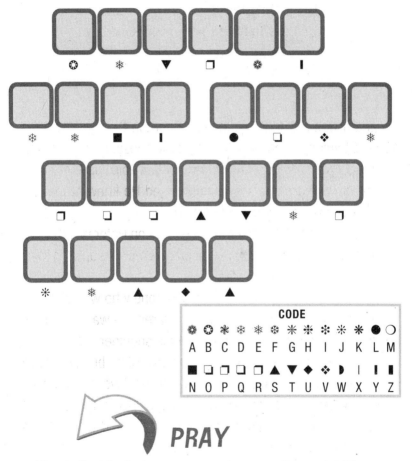

CODE

❂	✪	✳	❊	❋	❅	✺	❆	❉	❄	✳	●	○
A	B	C	D	E	F	G	H	I	J	K	L	M

■	❑	❐	❒	❐	▲	▼	◆	❖	◗	|	I	I
N	O	P	Q	R	S	T	U	V	W	X	Y	Z

PRAY

Thank God for loving us even when we disappoint Him and for allowing us to repent of our sin and follow Him.

44

Jesus Prays for His Followers

"But I have prayed for you that your faith may not fail. And you, when you have turned back, strengthen your brothers."
—Luke 22:32

Jesus knew that Simon Peter would soon turn his back on Jesus and deny that he knew Jesus. But Jesus also knew that, eventually, Peter would follow Him again and lead others to do the same. Jesus told Peter that He had prayed for Peter's future. He knew Peter would become a leader of the disciples after Jesus returned to heaven. Peter didn't understand what Jesus was telling him at the time.

As you read today's Bible verse, think about what Jesus was telling Peter. Jesus said that He had prayed for Peter. The Bible tells us that Jesus intercedes, or prays, for Christians. Jesus knew Peter's future, and He knows ours, too. How amazing to think that Jesus knows all these things, and He prays for our strength to do the right thing.

Challenge Accepted!

Romans 8:34 tells us that Jesus intercedes (prays) for believers. Copy Romans 8:34 here and write how knowing that Jesus prays for you helps you as you follow Him.

Romans 8:34

 **PRAY**

Thank Jesus for praying for you as you follow Him.

45

Following Jesus Can Be Hard

"Even if I have to die with you,"
Peter told him. "I will never deny you,"
and all the disciples said the same
thing.—Matthew 26:35

Destiny and her mom finished their daily Bible reading together. They had read about Jesus explaining that all His disciples would "fall away" or abandon Jesus that night. "How could Simon Peter and the other disciples abandon Jesus?" Destiny asked. "They knew Him better than anyone. They knew He was the Messiah!"

"It does seem hard to believe. But Jesus knew what they were all about to experience. It would be hard and scary. Jesus also knew that this was part of what was prophesied: His followers would scatter." Mom explained. "The good news is that Jesus also said that He would see them in Galilee after He had risen. He knew everything that was about to happen. As followers of Jesus, we want to think we would always do the right thing, honoring Jesus with our actions. Peter thought the same thing in verse 35. But the truth is, we all fail at some point. Thankfully, we have the example of Jesus and His disciples. We can know Jesus will forgive us and help us follow His way again."

Level Up!

Locate Matthew 26:31–35 in your Bible and read the same verses Destiny and her mom read. Circle some thing you think make it hard for people today to follow Jesus.

Friends who don't believe

Busy schedules

Feeling too tired for church

Being distracted by technology

Not understanding the Bible

Feeling bored in church

PRAY

Thank Jesus for His willingness to forgive
us even when we don't honor Him.

46

Stay Awake

*"Remain here and stay awake with
me."—Matthew 26:38*

After Jesus and His disciples finished their last meal together, they walked over to the garden of Gethsemane. It was getting late, but Jesus asked His disciples to wait there while He stepped away to pray. Jesus took Simon Peter, James, and John with Him farther into the garden and told them how troubled He was. He asked them to stay awake with Him. Then Jesus went a little farther by Himself and began to pray earnestly. Jesus knew He would soon be beaten and crucified, but He needed to pray to be sure this was the only way for salvation to come. If so, He was willing.

Jesus walked back to where Peter, James, and John were and found them sleeping. He asked them to stay awake and pray. Jesus did this three times and, each time, the disciples could not stay awake. Jesus had the strength to fight sadness and exhaustion to stay awake and talk to His Father, but His disciples didn't. They had fallen asleep. Finally, Jesus knew it was time. Judas was on his way with the soldiers who were coming to arrest Jesus.

Trivia Time!

The Garden of Gethsemane

- The garden of Gethsemane is a real place. You can still visit it today in Israel.

- The name "Gethsemane" means "olive press."

- Gethsemane was outside of Jerusalem on the Mount of Olives.

- Olive oil was and still is an important agricultural product in Israel.

- Gethsemane would have contained a grove of olive trees.

- Some of the olive trees on the Mount of Olives today are hundreds of years old.

 PRAY

Ask Jesus to give you His strength to pray no matter what you are going through. Tell Him what you are thinking about as you read about the lead-up to His crucifixion.

47

Keep Trying

"Stay awake and pray so that you won't enter into temptation. The spirit is willing, but the flesh is weak."—Mark 14:38

Jerome lay on his bed looking at the ceiling. He felt terrible. On Sunday, he listened to the Bible study and sang the songs. He was excited to be a new believer in Jesus and was sure he would always do the right thing from now on. But today, he spoke hatefully to his mom, cheated on a math test, and played video games so late he didn't have time to read his Bible. Now, he couldn't sleep. He started thinking about Sunday's Bible lesson. Jesus told Simon Peter to pray for himself so he would not give in to temptation. The pastor had explained that sometimes, even when we want to follow the way of Jesus, we fail.

"Jesus," Jerome prayed. "I messed up today. I'm sorry for my bad choices. Give me the courage to apologize to Mom and make the other things right, too. Please forgive me and help me to honor You with my actions tomorrow."

Let's Play!

Unscramble the words below to discover reasons we need to pray.

We pray for:

_____

SSIVEFRGONE

_____ TO DO THE _____ _____

SIWMOD   TGRHI   TGHNI

_____ TO _____ _____

GORACUE   KEAM   STGHNI

_____

IHTGR

 **PRAY**

Admit to Jesus the things you are sorry for. Thank Him for forgiving you and helping you to follow Him.

48

Put Away Your Sword

Then Simon Peter, who had a sword, drew it, struck the high priest's servant.—John 18:10

Mason was reading the book of John in his Bible when he saw something that surprised him. As the soldiers came to arrest Jesus, Simon Peter drew his sword. A disciple had a sword!? This sounded like something from an action movie. Peter hit the high priest's servant and cut off his right ear! As Mason thought about what he read, he realized that Peter seemed to think of himself as Jesus's protector. He thought he might have done the same thing. He loved action-packed good-guy-bad-guy scenes. But the more Mason thought about it, he remembered how Jesus didn't need protecting.

Jesus knew all the things were happening for a reason. If Jesus wanted to cut off that man's ear, he could have just looked at it! He didn't need Peter's sword. The disciples still did not understand what was about to happen, but Jesus did. Jesus didn't need Peter or any other person to save Him at all. He is the true hero of every story. He is always in control, and He always does what's best.

Level Up!

Have you ever read the events surrounding Jesus's arrest? Did you know about Peter's sword? Locate and read John 18:1–12. Write the words from John 18:7 in the spiral below.

PRAY

Thank God for Jesus, who doesn't need anyone to protect Him but came to protect you. If you're scared or worried, tell Him, and ask Him to help you trust His protection.

49

Abandoned

"But all this has happened so that the writings of the prophets would be fulfilled." Then all the disciples deserted him and ran away.—Matthew 26:56

How do you think you would have felt if you were standing there when Jesus was arrested? As the soldiers tied Jesus's hands and surrounded Him to take Him away, would you have been afraid they'd arrest you, too? Simon Peter tried to defend Jesus, but Jesus told him not to. It must have all felt so strange and terrifying. But everything happened just like the prophets in the Old Testament had written.

God told men long ago what to write, and now it was coming true. It was hard for the disciples to understand that Scripture was being fulfilled. They ran and hid. Eventually, two of the disciples circled back to see where the soldiers took Jesus and what happened. At that moment, Jesus was alone. His followers abandoned Him. But Jesus didn't get scared and run away—He didn't abandon what His Father called Him to. Jesus loved us enough to finish what He came to do.

Level Up!

Peter thought he would never leave Jesus, but he did. Read Matthew 26:55–56 again and take it to the next level by thinking about these questions.

Why do you think Peter abandoned Jesus?

What do you think you would have done?

 PRAY

Ask Jesus to help you know that because He died on the cross, you will never be abandoned. Thank Him for experiencing so much pain so you wouldn't have to.

50

Two Disciples Follow

Simon Peter was following Jesus, as was another disciple.—John 18:15

Madi was spending Easter weekend with her Gram. One of Gram's traditions was reading about the events that led up to Easter Sunday. They read about the night Jesus was arrested. Gram read about Simon Peter and another disciple following Jesus to the high priest's courtyard. "Didn't the disciples run away because they were afraid?" Madi asked.

"Good memory!" Gram said. "Peter and John came back to see what happened to Jesus, but the soldiers had taken Jesus to the courtyard of the priest. Courtyards were walled in, and you had to enter through a doorway like a gate. John realized Peter was outside and he asked the girl who was the doorkeeper to let Peter in. That way they both could see what was happening to Jesus."

"And since John wrote this story, he's describing exactly what he saw!" Madi exclaimed. Gram smiled. She loved hearing how God's Word was sinking into her granddaughter's heart.

Let's Play!

Solve the crossword, then think about what each word has to do with the events you read about today.

Across

2. The disciple other than Peter
4. Could not get into the courtyard at first
5. A girl had this job
6. Two disciples followed to see what would happen to _____.

Down

1. John helped Peter gain entrance here
3. The courtyard belonged to this person

Word Bank: COURTYARD PETER GATEKEEPER JOHN HIGH PRIEST JESUS

PRAY

Thank God for the Bible, which tells us exactly what happened when Jesus died. Thank Him that death of Jesus washed away your sins.

51

The Rooster Crowed

Immediately a rooster crowed a second time, and Peter remembered when Jesus had spoken the word to him, "Before the rooster crows twice, you will deny me three times." And he broke down and wept.—Mark 14:72

Simon Peter was one of the first disciples chosen by Jesus to follow Him. He was in the inner circle of three who accompanied Jesus at special times. Peter boldly declared his intention to follow Jesus no matter what. He even tried to protect Jesus by attacking the high priest's servant with a sword when Jesus was arrested. And yet, as Jesus was led away, Peter feared.

Peter followed Jesus to the courtyard of the high priest and watched from a distance to see what would happen. In that courtyard, Peter was asked three different times if he was a Jesus follower. Each time, Peter answered with more agitation, "No!" When the rooster crowed, Peter realized it had happened as Jesus said it would. He looked up and saw Jesus looking at him and broke down crying as he left. Peter had done what he never thought he would do. He denied Jesus.

Challenge Accepted!

Have you ever read about the events that happened when Peter denied knowing Jesus? Locate Mark 14:66–72 and read what happened. Draw a picture of a scene from the story.

 **PRAY**

Thank God that He loves you even when even when your faith is weak. Tell God you are sorry and ask Him to forgive you.

52

John Wrote about
What He Saw

*Then he said to the disciple, "Here is your
mother." And from that hour the disciple
took her into his home.—John 19:27*

Carter trusted Jesus as his Savior a few weeks ago, and
his pastor suggested that he begin a habit of Bible reading.
Carter's pastor encouraged him to read the Gospel of John,
a chapter or two a day, to get in the practice of daily Bible
reading. He enjoyed reading the things John wrote. His
pastor told him that John was one of the chosen disciples
and was there when everything he wrote about happened.
That made it extra interesting to Carter.

He felt sad as he read about Jesus's crucifixion. He was
amazed that Jesus told John to take care of His mother
Mary, and John did. Even when Jesus should have been
most concerned for Himself, He protected and provided for
others. Carter wrote a prayer in his journal, "Jesus, thank
You for the ways You show how much You care for others.
Thank You that You love and care for me, too."

Level Up!

The Gospel of John was written by the apostle John, one of Jesus's twelve chosen disciples. When you read his Gospel, you are reading the words of someone who was there. He saw Jesus and listened to His teachings. Answer this in the blank space: Why do you think it was important for God to include Bible writers who saw things firsthand?

 **PRAY**

Praise Jesus that He cares for and loves you.
Tell Him what His love means to you.

53

Joseph of Arimathea

Joseph of Arimathea, a prominent member of the Sanhedrin who was himself looking forward to the kingdom of God, came and boldly went to Pilate and asked for Jesus's body.—Mark 15:43

Jesus's disciples all left when He died. Most of them were in hiding because they were afraid, and only a couple of women stayed to see what would happen.

God always has a plan. Through one of His prophets, God said His plan was that Jesus would die with the wicked but be with a rich man in His death (Isaiah 53:9). This prophecy was fulfilled through Joseph of Arimathea, a wealthy and important religious leader who had been carefully listening to Jesus's teaching. After Jesus died, Joseph asked Pilate for permission to care for Jesus's body.

Jewish tradition was to place a body in a tomb after death, and Joseph had recently paid to have a new tomb dug out of a nearby rock. Jesus's body was placed in the brand-new tomb of a rich man, just like the prophet said. Joseph worked quickly. He rolled a large stone over the opening to protect Jesus's body before the Sabbath began at sundown.

Trivia Time!

All four Gospels mention Joseph of Arimathea. Look up each verse to find out a fact about Joseph of Arimathea. The first letter of the missing word in each sentence has been provided for you.

Matthew 27:57: Joseph of Arimathea was r_____.

Mark 15:46: Joseph of Arimathea wrapped Jesus's body in l_____ cloth.

Luke 23:50: Joseph of Arimathea was a member of the S_____.

John 19:39: N_____ help Joseph care for Jesus's body by bringing burial spices.

 PRAY

Thank God for all the people who helped during this sad time. Thank God for people who help you during sad times.

54

The Women

Mary Magdalene and Mary the mother of Joses were watching where he was laid.—Mark 15:47

I wish women were more important in the Bible," Kelsey sighed as she and her mom set the table for dinner.

Mom smiled. "Well then, I have some good news for you! There are lots of women who do important things all through the Bible! In fact, even though the disciples left when Jesus was arrested and crucified, it was a small group of women who stayed and watched everything unfold. They saw where Jesus's body was placed so they could go take care of Him after the Sabbath was over. Because they made sure to see everything that happened, we have great eye-witness accounts of Jesus's death, burial, and resurrection!"

"Oh, I didn't know that part," Kelsey said. "Maybe I just hadn't noticed before. After dinner, I'm going to go back and read those parts again. I wonder what else I missed!"

Let's Play!

Follow the maze to discover the place the women went.

 **PRAY**

*Thank God for all the details He included
in His Word. Ask Him to help you discover
something new each time you read your Bible.*

55

Unexpected

So she went running to Simon Peter and to the other disciple, the one Jesus loved, and said to them, "They've taken the Lord out of the tomb, and we don't know where they've put him!"—John 20:2

What's the most surprising thing you've ever seen? Was it surprising because it was unexpected or surprising because it was exciting? Maybe it was a funny-looking animal at the zoo or your parents surprising you with a weekend vacation. When the women went to the empty tomb early on the first day of the week, they expected to need help moving the huge stone. They expected to find Jesus's body. What they found was amazingly unexpected.

The stone had been rolled away, and the tomb was empty! Mary Magdalene thought someone took Jesus's body. She ran to find Peter and John. She said, "They've taken the Lord out of the tomb, and we don't know where they've put him!" She was upset. She wanted answers. She hoped the disciples would help her find out what had happened. She didn't know at that moment, but she would soon find out she didn't have a reason to be upset. She had a reason to celebrate.

Level Up!

Read John 20: 1–2 and answer the following questions.

Why do you think Mary was confused?

What had Jesus told them would happen?

Why do you think they didn't understand yet that Jesus had risen?

 **PRAY**

Ask God to help you trust Him when you don't understand what is happening. T hank Him that He is always in control.

56

Racing to See

Then, following him, Simon Peter also came. He entered the tomb and saw the linen cloths lying there.—John 20:6

How is your study of Simon Peter's life going?" Mom asked Logan as he worked on his report.

"It's been more interesting than I expected," Logan replied. "I started by looking up all the places Peter is mentioned, then all the places it mentions the disciples, since he was part of that group. One cool thing I learned is that Peter and John were two of the disciples who saw the most firsthand. Today, I read about how they raced to the tomb after Mary told them it was empty. John wrote about it in his Gospel. I think it's funny that he said he outran Peter. But when they got there, John stopped at the opening, and Peter went right on in!"

Mom laughed, "It sounds like they were normal guys, kind of like you and your friends! And it must have been amazing to be the first to see the cloth lying there where Jesus had been."

"Or scary!" Logan remarked. "They weren't sure what had happened yet!"

Let's Play!

Unscramble the words to complete the sentences.

Mary told the disciples that the tomb was _____.

PTYME

Peter and John _____ to the tomb.

CARDE

_____ got there first.

HNOJ

But _____ ran into the tomb first.

EERTP

 PRAY

*Thank God for using regular people to do
His amazing work. Ask Him to show you
the amazing things He has for you to do.*

57

He's Alive!

Mary Magdalene went and announced to the disciples, "I have seen the Lord!"—John 20:18

Mary Magdalene was in the group of women who found the tomb empty. She raced to tell the disciples. Peter and John ran to the tomb and also saw that it was empty. Then they left. Mary stayed near the tomb when angels appeared, saying Jesus had risen. Mary was so confused; she was still afraid someone had stolen Jesus's body. She was crying when she saw a person nearby.

Maybe it was the gardener. She asked where they had taken the body. Then the man said her name, and instantly, Mary realized it was Jesus. He *was* alive! "Teacher!" she said in amazement. Jesus was truly there. She could touch Him! Jesus told her to go tell the disciples. Mary raced to find them and give them the good news. "I have seen the Lord!" she exclaimed.

Level Up!

Locate John 20:11–18 in your Bible and read about the events for yourself. Write about how you would have felt if you had been there with Mary.

 **PRAY**

Ask God to help you feel the same excitement Mary felt when you think about how Jesus rose from the dead.

58

Unsuspecting Travelers

*Then beginning with Moses and all
the Prophets, he interpreted for them
the things concerning himself in all
the Scriptures.—Luke 24:27*

When Jesus rose from the dead, you might have expected a thundering announcement from heaven or an immediate appearance to the disciples. However, on this amazing day, Jesus first appeared to Mary Magdalene in the garden, Peter, and two unsuspecting followers of Jesus. These men were the first to have a long conversation with Him.

One man's name was Cleopas, but the Bible doesn't tell us the name of the other. Like Mary, the men didn't recognize Jesus at first, but during the seven-mile walk from Jerusalem to Emmaus, Jesus explained what the Old Testament said would happen to the Messiah. What a Bible study that must have been! It wasn't until they stopped for supper that Jesus allowed the two followers to know who He was. As soon as they realized it was Jesus, He disappeared!

Let's Play!

Can you find these words from today's devotion in the word search?

```
S  C  R  I  P  T  U  R  E  A
I  M  P  K  M  W  B  X  N  S
Q  A  E  R  O  B  X  B  N  Q
Z  R  T  T  S  P  M  U  J  J
E  Y  E  W  E  O  M  E  L  E
J  E  R  U  S  A  L  E  M  M
E  P  R  O  P  H  E  T  S  M
S  W  T  U  L  M  M  T  W  A
U  O  U  U  O  A  E  D  K  U
S  I  W  C  L  E  O  P  A  S
```

Word Bank: SCRIPTURE   JERUSALEM   PROPHETS   CLEOPAS
JESUS   EMMAUS   PETER   MOSES   MARY

 **PRAY**

*Thank God for the many ways He helps
you understand Scripture.*

59

Hard to Believe!

But while they still were amazed and in disbelief because of their joy, he asked them, "Do you have anything here to eat?"—Luke 24:41

Does God get mad when we ask questions?" Mia asked her dad.

"Not at all." Dad assured her. "God made us. He gave us the ability to think and wonder. I believe He likes it when we want to know the truth and ask questions."

"Sometimes I know what the answer is supposed to be, but I still have a hard time really understanding," Mia admitted.

"The disciples experienced the same thing," Dad said. Mia looked confused, so Dad continued. "The day Jesus rose from the dead, there were reports from Mary, Peter, and two other followers about seeing Jesus. Then, Jesus appeared in the room with them, and they knew the door was locked! They were amazed, surprised, and so excited they could hardly believe what was happening."

Challenge Accepted!

Think about these questions and write down your thoughts.

Why did the disciples have a hard time believing Jesus was alive even though several people said they had seen Him?

Do you believe Jesus is alive? What helps you know this is true?

PRAY

Ask God to show you the answers to your questions in His Word and through other Christians.

60

Thomas's Turn

A week later his disciples were indoors again, and Thomas was with them. Even though the doors were locked, Jesus came and stood among them and said, "Peace be with you."—John 20:26

Thomas was one of the original twelve disciples. The Bible does not say why, but when Jesus appeared to His disciples in the locked room the first time, Thomas wasn't there, and he did not believe what the others had to say. He even said that he wouldn't believe unless he could touch the scars on Jesus's hands and feet. Jesus first appeared to the disciples the day He was resurrected.

One week later, the disciples were again in a room with the door shut and locked. This time Thomas was with them. Jesus greeted them as before, "Peace be with you." Then, before Thomas could say anything, Jesus offered to let Thomas touch the scars. Thomas exclaimed, "My Lord and my God!" Jesus told Thomas that he believed because he saw, but people who believed without seeing Jesus in person are blessed. That's us!

Level Up!

Compare the two passages and fill in the chart.

- Luke 24:36–49 describes the first time Jesus appeared to the group of disciples.

- John 20:24–29 describes the next time one week later.

	Luke 24:36–49	John 20:24–29
Who had a hard time believing?		
Where were they?		
What was the first thing Jesus said when He appeared?		
What did Jesus do to prove He was really alive?		

PRAY

Ask Jesus to help you believe even though you haven't seen Him.

61

Go Fish . . . Again!

*After this, Jesus revealed himself
again to his disciples by the
Sea of Tiberias.—John 21:1*

Ella decided to make a list of the times Jesus appeared to people after His resurrection. She read about the first two times Jesus appeared to His disciples. Both times Jesus appeared in the room even though the door was shut and locked. When she read about Jesus's third appearance to His disciples, she noticed that only seven of them were together—Simon Peter, Thomas, Nathanael, James, John, and two others.

Peter decided he was going fishing. Ella wondered if Peter was a person who couldn't sit still and needed something to do or if he just needed to catch fish since that was his family business. The seven men fished all night and caught nothing. The next morning a man on the shore told them to cast the net on the right side of the boat. They did and caught so many fish, they couldn't haul them in. That was when John recognized the man on the shore and said to Peter, "It is the Lord!" They didn't know Jesus was nearby, but He was still with them.

Let's Play!

Do you remember who went fishing? Use the code to solve for the names of the disciples who went fishing.

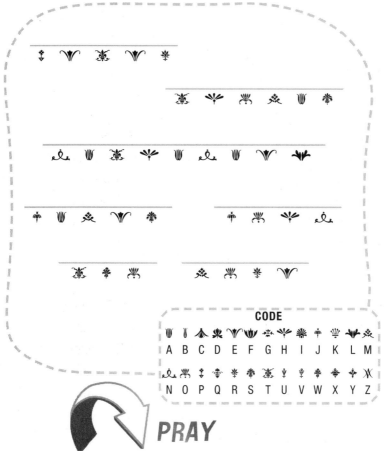

CODE

A	B	C	D	E	F	G	H	I	J	K	L	M

N	O	P	Q	R	S	T	U	V	W	X	Y	Z

PRAY

Thank God that He is always near whether you think about Him or not.

62

Another Amazing Catch of Fish

When Simon Peter heard that it was the Lord,
he tied his outer clothing around him
(for he had taken it off) and plunged
into the sea.—John 21:7

What do you know about Simon Peter so far? Peter followed Jesus as soon as Jesus asked him to. He saw the miracles Jesus did and listened to what Jesus taught. He spoke boldly many times and got in trouble for some of the things he said. He tried to defend Jesus when Jesus was arrested, then only a few hours later, he denied that he even knew Jesus. Peter saw the resurrected Jesus more than once.

Now he spent the night fishing and caught nothing. When the man on the shore told them to throw the nets on the other side of the boat, do you wonder if Peter did it because he was too tired to argue or because he was beginning to remember another time this happened? Either way, as soon as John recognized Jesus and told Peter, Peter had one focus. He wanted to get to Jesus! He plunged into the sea and waded up on shore where Jesus was cooking a breakfast of fish.

Level Up!

You can read the whole story from today's devotion in John 21:1–19. Think about these questions:

1. In this passage, the disciples caught so many fish they could not haul the net into the boat. What other time did some of these disciples see a miraculous catch of fish?

2. Peter plunged into the water to get to Jesus. What other time did Peter try to go to Jesus on the water?

3. Peter joined Jesus on shore where Jesus had a charcoal fire going. Where was Peter recently standing by a fire?

4. Peter denied knowing Jesus three times. Did you read something in this passage that also happened three times?

 **PRAY**

Thank God for loving you and helping you in the challenging times and in the good times.

63
Restored

Peter was grieved that he asked him the third time, "Do you love me?"
He said, "Lord, you know everything; you know that I love you." "Feed my sheep," Jesus said.—John 21:17

Ryan knew he hurt his Aunt Nancy's feelings when he ignored her at his baseball game. She cheered for him and stayed through the whole game. But afterward, when the team raced over to grab their after-game treat, he didn't even look her way.

When Aunt Nancy came over for dinner that night, Ryan thought she might ignore him the way he ignored her. Instead, when she arrived, she gave Ryan a huge hug and told him how proud she was of the way he played.

"Aunt Nancy, I'm sorry I was rude to you. I was afraid of what my friends might think. I should have at least smiled and waved at you." Aunt Nancy just gave Ryan another hug as she smiled. Ryan knew he was forgiven.

Peter had denied knowing Jesus three times, but after eating breakfast on the seashore, Jesus gave Peter three opportunities to say he loved Jesus. Jesus let Peter know there was still work for Peter to do and he was forgiven.

Challenge Accepted!

Do you ever feel like you've disappointed God? Remember that He knows you better than anyone else, and He loves you no matter what. Write a prayer to God telling Him why you want to obey Him and honor Him with your words and actions.

PRAY

Thank God that He is patient with us and loves us even when we let Him down.

64

Visible Proof

*And that he appeared to Cephas, then
to the Twelve.—1 Corinthians 15:5*

"Who was Cephas?" Nora asked Mrs. Emily as they read
the Bible on Sunday.

"Cephas is Peter! It's the same person. Cephas is his
name in a language called Aramaic, and Peter is his name
in Greek. They both refer to a rock." Mrs. Emily explained.
"Jesus knew that Peter would become a rock-solid leader
of the church after Jesus's resurrection. He is also the one
who first confessed that Jesus was the Messiah—and
Jesus said that belief was the rock on which He would
build His church. Peter's name was a reminder of these
things."

"So, Cephas, or Peter, saw Jesus *after* He was resurrected?" Nora asked.

"Yes, Peter saw and spoke with Jesus on a few occa-
sions. In fact, one time Jesus appeared to a group of
more than 500 believers at the same time. Many people
saw Jesus, which proves Jesus was resurrected. We can
believe it!" Mrs. Emily assured Nora.

Trivia Time!

Complete the trivia facts by finding the missing information in 1 Corinthians 15:3–8 and filling in the blanks. Did you know Paul wrote 1 Corinthians as a letter to the believers in Corinth?

1. Paul told the Corinthians two things Jesus did that fulfilled what the Scriptures said would happen. They were:_____ according to the Scriptures, and

_____ according to the Scriptures.

2. How many people did Paul list that the resurrected Jesus appeared to:

C_____
The T_____
Over _____
J_____
All the A_____
M__ (Paul)

PRAY

Thank God for the many witnesses who proved Jesus is alive.

65

Go, Make Disciples

*"Go, therefore, and make disciples
of all nations."—Matthew 28:19*

Jesus spent forty days on earth after His resurrection. He appeared to individuals and groups of people. Several times, He appeared to His disciples. Jesus spent the time giving His disciples final instructions. Matthew 28:19–20 is called the Great Commission. A commission is a command to act in a certain way or to perform a specific duty. Jesus told His disciples to tell the nations about Him.

That means Jesus wants us to take the good news about Him to people everywhere, from every people group. A people group is a group of people that speaks the same language and are of the same ethnicity. Jesus came to save people who look differently, speak differently, and have different backgrounds. His kingdom is beautifully diverse! Jesus was asking His followers to share the gospel then, now, and in the future. That means it was the twelve disciples' call then, and it's your call now!

Let's Play!

Across

3. Jesus gave the command to His _____.
4. One of the first acts of obedience by a new believer.
6. Jesus said to go and make disciples of all _____.

Down

1. A command to act a certain way or perform a duty
2. Jesus's last command to His disciples is called the _____ Commission.
5. _____ commanded the disciples to baptize in the name of the Father and the Son and the Holy Spirit.

Word Bank: GREAT   JESUS   COMMISSION   DISCIPLES   BAPTISM   NATIONS

PRAY

*Ask God to help you obey
Jesus's Great Commission.*

66

Power Promised

But you will receive power when the Holy Spirit has come on you.—Acts 1:8

The book of Acts was written by Luke who also wrote the Gospel of Luke. Luke wrote both books to his friend, Theophilus. He wanted to carefully compile all the facts and evidence about Jesus. Luke's Gospel was written about all the things Jesus came to teach and to do. In Acts, Luke described what took place with Jesus's final instructions to His disciples and the beginning of the early church.

Luke wrote that Jesus appeared many times over the course of forty days, providing many "convincing proofs" before He returned to heaven. Jesus also promised the Holy Spirit would come in a few days and give the disciples the power to be witnesses for Him. Jesus's disciples shared the good news of Jesus in all of Judea, Samaria, and to the ends of the earth.

Level Up!

The Great Commission (Matthew 28:19–20) and Acts 1:8 contain important final messages from Jesus before He returned to heaven. Read both verses from your Bible and list the things that are similar in each.

 **PRAY**

Thank the Holy Spirit for helping believers do the things God sends them to do.

67

Jesus Ascended

After he had said this, he was taken up as they were watching, and a cloud took him out of their sight.—Acts 1:9

Austin described the events that took place when Jesus ascended into heaven to his discipleship group of elementary school boys. The boys leaned forward as they listened to the amazing details. Austin described how a cloud took Jesus into the sky and out of sight while the disciples watched. He described how two men in white robes appeared and asked why they were gazing at the sky. The idea of two men in white robes made the boys laugh. Then Austin shared that the men told the disciples that Jesus would return someday in the exact way He left.

"So, Jesus came back?" Jay asked, surprised.

"Not yet, but He will! Do you want to know what the disciples did next?" Austin asked before the boys nodded in excitement. "The disciples went back to Jerusalem to wait, just like Jesus told them to. They kept praying while they waited. That's something we can do. We can pray and continue to honor Jesus with our actions until He returns. Remember, God is always in control, and His way is always best. Jesus promised to come back in God's perfect time."

Challenge Accepted!

After everything that happened, how do you think seeing Jesus's ascension helped the disciples and their belief?

Would you liked to have been there to see Jesus ascend? Why?

PRAY

Ask God to help you honor Jesus in your thoughts, words, and actions until He returns.

68

A New Number Twelve

In those days Peter stood up among the brothers and sisters—the number of people who were together was about a hundred and twenty.—Acts 1:15

After Jesus ascended, Peter stepped up to lead the group of believers, just like Jesus said he would. At that time, there were about 120 altogether. Peter's first action step was to replace Judas. Peter reminded the group that Judas's role in Jesus's arrest was prophesied in the Psalms. Now it was time to choose a replacement who would follow Jesus's commands and teachings.

Peter guided the group to choose from among the men who had been following Jesus from the time John the Baptist baptized Him until the day of His ascension. Two men fit the requirements. The group prayed to know which man God would choose. Matthias was selected, and he joined the other eleven apostles. After that, the apostles and other believers had to wait for the fulfillment of Jesus's promise to send a Helper. Peter and the others waited and prayed.

Let's Play!

Can you find these words in the word search?

Word Bank: PETER BELIEVERS PSALMS PRAYED
MATTHIAS ELEVEN APOSTLES WAITED

```
N  B  E  L  I  E  V  E  R  S
W  A  P  O  S  T  L  E  S  E
E  X  V  W  K  H  W  Y  P  R
L  T  O  P  E  V  D  S  E  W
E  G  R  B  S  K  M  V  T  A
V  H  J  S  C  A  O  O  E  I
E  F  Z  Z  T  V  L  Y  R  T
N  L  M  Z  N  X  D  M  R  E
M  M  A  T  T  H  I  A  S  D
T  J  V  J  P  R  A  Y  E  D
```

 **PRAY**

*Thank God for the leaders in your church who
help people know how to seek God's will.*

69

Empowered

Suddenly a sound like that of a violent rushing wind came from heaven, and it filled the whole house where they were staying.—Acts 2:2

Lucy brought her new word list from Kid's ministry to her mom. "What does *Pentecost* mean?" she asked. Lucy's mom had just learned about Pentecost in her own Sunday school class.

"The first part *pente* means fifty. For Christians, Pentecost was fifty days after Jesus's resurrection. The apostles and other believers were together in a room when the Holy Spirit gave them the power to do the things God wanted them to do."

"What kind of things?" Lucy asked.

"Well, do you remember how Jesus gave His disciples the Great Commission, telling them to make disciples of all the people groups in the world? They wouldn't be able to do that by themselves. They needed God's help! So the Holy Spirit, who is God just like God the Father and God the Son, came to empower them for this task. And He is still empowering the church for this task now!" Mom explained.

"Wow, that's power!" Lucy exclaimed. "I'm glad God gives us what we need to do the jobs He wants us to do."

Challenge Accepted!

What are some ways people today hear about Jesus? List as many ways as you can think of. Don't forget about travel and technology.

PRAY

Thank God for all the ways He helps people tell others about Him.

70

Peter Takes the Lead

Therefore let all the house of Israel know with certainty that God has made this Jesus, whom you crucified, both Lord and Messiah.—Acts 2:36

When the Holy Spirit came upon the group of believers, the sound of the wind was so loud that a crowd gathered to see what was happening. Peter stepped up to take the lead and spoke to the crowd. "Let me explain this to you; pay attention to my words," Peter began. Then Peter quoted verses from the prophets (books we have in the Old Testament) to explain who Jesus is and why He came. Peter quoted from the prophet Joel and from several of the psalms that prophesied about the Messiah.

The more Peter spoke, the more the people knew in their hearts that he was telling the truth. The people in the crowd asked what they needed to do. Peter told them to repent of their sin, believe in Jesus, and be baptized to publicly show they chose to follow Jesus. God used Peter's leadership to tell people the good news that day and to grow His church even more.

Trivia Time!

You can read about Peter's sermon in Acts 2:14–41.

Peter used passages we can find in:
- Joel 2:28–32
- Psalm 16:8–11
- Psalm 110:1

About 3,000 people became believers that day.

Pentecost happened fifty days after Jesus's resurrection.

 **PRAY**

Ask God to help you understand more about what it means to follow Jesus.

71

Ready!

But Peter said, "I don't have silver or gold, but what I do have, I give you: In the name of Jesus Christ of Nazareth, get up and walk!"—Acts 3:6

Dylan's dad challenged him to read the book of Acts to learn about how the early church started. Dylan read about the day of Pentecost, when the Holy Spirit empowered the believers to speak boldly about Jesus. When Dylan began reading chapter 3, he was amazed. One day, as Peter and John went to the temple to pray, they passed a man who could not walk. The man had to beg for money. Peter said they didn't have money, but in the name of Jesus, Peter told the man to get up and walk. The man was healed instantly!

The man entered the temple walking, leaping, and praising God! The people who saw it were astonished. God had done something even better than the man could have ever imagined. God is always in control, and His way is always best! Peter took the opportunity to tell the listening crowd about Jesus. Peter was always ready to share the good news about Jesus whenever he could.

Level Up!

Have you read how the early church started? You can read about it in the book of Acts. If you'd like to read about the events from today's devotional, check out Acts 3 for yourself.

List some facts from the story that you find interesting.

 **PRAY**

Ask God to help you be like Peter and always be ready to share the good news of Jesus with others.

72

Growing Numbers

But many of those who heard the message believed, and the number of the men came to about five thousand.—Acts 4:4

In the previous devotion, you read about Peter healing a man who couldn't walk. After the man was healed, a large crowd gathered, and Peter preached to the crowd about Jesus. You would think the people would have been glad to hear Peter's message. Instead, some of the temple officials confronted Peter and John for preaching about Jesus and His resurrection.

The officials brought the captain of the temple police, and they took Peter and John into custody and held them until the next day since it was already getting late. However, even though Peter and John were locked away, people in the crowd kept thinking about what Peter said. Many of them became believers in Jesus. In fact, after Peter's sermon, the number of men who were now believers came to about five thousand.

Let's Play!

Solve the math equations, then see if you can remember which number goes in the correct blank.

10 x 10 x 30 = _____

(250 divided by 2) − 5 = _____

3,000 + 120 + 1,880 = _____

_____ = Number of disciples and followers that were together when the Holy Spirit came.

_____ = Number of people who became believers and were baptized on Pentecost.

_____ = Number of believers after Peter preached to outside the temple.

 **PRAY**

Ask God to help you have the courage to tell others about Him even if they don't seem to listen at first.

73

Can't Stop Speaking

Peter and John answered them, "Whether it's right in the sight of God for us to listen to you rather than to God, you decide; for we are unable to stop speaking about what we have seen and heard."—Acts 4:19–20

Mom," Marissa said after school one day, "Rylee said I shouldn't talk about Jesus at school. But Julia asked me a question about Jesus, so I answered. Did I do something wrong?"

"No, of course not," Mom assured Marissa. "The Bible tells us to always be ready to give an answer about what we believe. We need to remember that God calls every person to believe Him individually, and if another person doesn't believe in Jesus, we shouldn't get angry or be mean to them. We should simply pray that God will work in their lives. Do you remember Pastor Rich talking about the disciples in his sermon on Sunday? The religious leaders tried to make Peter and John stop preaching about Jesus, but the disciples said they couldn't stop speaking about what they had seen and heard."

"I want to be like the disciples!" Maria exclaimed. "I love Jesus, and I really want my friends to know about Him. I can't stop talking about Him, especially when they ask."

Trivia Time!

Who were those people?

Peter and John were brought before a huge group of powerful people (Acts 4:5–6).

- Annas: the high priest at that time
- Caiaphas: Annas's father-in-law. Caiaphas had been high priest before Annas was. Caiaphas still maintained a good deal of power.
- All the members of the high priestly family
- Sanhedrin: a group of Jewish leaders that served as legal counsel. There were seventy-one members, including the high priest. It included Pharisees and Sadducees.
- Pharisees: religious leaders whose name means "separated." They taught the law, and most did not like Jesus.
- Sadducees: religious leaders who came from wealthy and high priestly families. They did not believe in life after death (resurrection), angels, or demons.

PRAY

Ask God to help you know how to use kind words to tell others about Him.

74

Community

Now the entire group of those who believed were of one heart and mind, and no one claimed that any of his possessions was his own, but instead they held everything in common.—Acts 4:32

Parker helped Carlos, his mission group leader, carry the last of the boxes to the church van. The boys and their leaders were about to take a load of food and other supplies to the local family center. They spent the afternoon helping organize the rooms with food and clothes and planting flowers by the front walk.

"Doing things like this makes me feel really glad inside," Parker said.

"It feels good because this is the way God planned for us to help each other," Carlos replied. "The early church began by helping each other and making sure everyone's needs were met. Jesus taught us to serve others. That's what community really means. Serving others helps us show them what the love of God looks like."

Let's Play!

Simple Gomoku

Communities do things together like play a game. Try this game with a friend using this grid or draw a bigger one on a sheet of paper. You will need buttons or small circles of paper in two colors.

To play: Players take turns placing their color of paper on the board anywhere lines cross. The goal is to be the first to get five pieces in a row in any direction and to block your opponent from getting five in a row. Look up "How to play Gomoku" online if you need additional help!

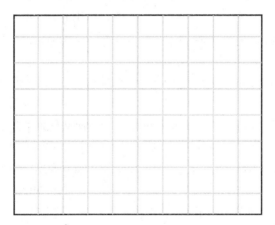

 PRAY

Ask God to help you think of ways to show kindness to people you know in ways that please God.

75

Signs & Wonders

Many signs and wonders were being done among the people through the hands of the apostles. They were all together in Solomon's Colonnade.—Acts 5:12

Solomon's Colonnade was a raised outer part of the temple where Peter recently healed a man who couldn't walk. He and John had preached there once and were then arrested. But that didn't stop them. They continued to gather in that same place, Solomon's Colonnade! The apostles preached the good news about Jesus.

The Bible says that "multitudes of both men and women" became believers. The Holy Spirit was truly the Helper Jesus promised the apostles He would send. Through the power of the Holy Spirit, the apostles provided healing for many who were sick. The apostles knew that it was not them; God was working through them to do wonders and signs so people would believe in Jesus.

Challenge Accepted!

What things have you seen or read about that help you believe in the power of God?

Why do you think others don't believe in God?

 **PRAY**

Ask God to help you recognize the amazing things He does for you.

76
Jail Again

Peter and the apostles replied,
"We must obey God rather
than people."—Acts 5:29

Peter and John had already been in jail for telling people about Jesus, but they continued to preach. The high priest and the Sadducees were jealous of how many people believed what the apostles said. So they had the apostles thrown in jail again! During the night an angel of the Lord opened the prison doors and told the apostles to go back to the temple and keep preaching.

The next morning the jail doors were locked, the guards were standing at the doors, but the apostles were gone! Someone came and told the high priest and Sadducees that the apostles were back at the temple. They sent the commander of the temple police to bring the apostles to stand before the Sanhedrin. Peter and the apostles explained that they had to obey God and that Jesus was the promised One sent to be Savior.

Level Up!

Today's devotion is like a court room drama. Read Acts 5:17–42 and write or draw the parts that stand out to you.

 **PRAY**

Ask God to help you have the courage of the apostles as you tell others about Him.

77

Help Needed

The Twelve summoned the whole company of the disciples and said, "It would not be right for us to give up preaching the word of God to wait on tables."—Acts 6:2

Mr. Bruce visited Ayla's family to introduce himself as their family deacon for the new year. He explained that if they had needs or prayer concerns, they could call him, especially when the pastor might not be available. After he left, Ayla asked her dad if Mr. Bruce was like a preacher. "Not really," Dad explained. "Our church wants to make everyone feel cared for, and that's too much for just one person, so we have deacons. In the early church, the apostles set up deacons so they would have time to pray, study, and prepare their teaching. Our church still does the same thing."

"Can anyone be a deacon?" Ayla asked.

"A deacon is someone with a strong, growing relationship with the Lord," Dad said. "In fact, the Bible gives a list of qualifications for a deacon."

Ayla smiled. "Well, I like Mr. Bruce. I'm glad the apostles had that idea all those years ago."

Trivia Time!

The early church chose seven men to be the first deacons. We don't know much about these seven men. We do know:

- Stephen boldly preached the gospel and was eventually killed, while Paul, who later became a believer, was standing there.
- Philip traveled to preach in Samaria, and many became believers. He explained the gospel to a man from Ethiopia who was traveling on his way back home. The man also became a believer.

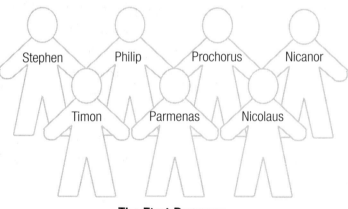

The First Deacons

 PRAY

Thank God for the pastors in your church and for the deacons and others who help take care of people.

78

Cornelius

Now send men to Joppa and call for Simon, who is also named Peter.—Acts 10:5

Today, we'll read part one of a three-part story. Acts 10 introduces us to a Roman Centurion who lived in Caesarea. His name was Cornelius. Jesus had explained that salvation is for both Jewish people and Gentile people. (Gentiles are people who aren't Jewish.) However, the disciples still did not fully understand. Roman soldiers often mistreated the Jewish people and made them pay fees that were unfair. Cornelius was different.

He believed in God, and he was known for the charitable things he did for the local Jewish people. Cornelius prayed to God every day. One day when Cornelius was praying, he saw an angel of God who told him that God was pleased with his kindness and his prayers. The angel told Cornelius to send for a man named Peter who was in Joppa. Cornelius immediately obeyed God and sent two of his trusted servants and a devoted soldier to go find Peter. God saw Cornelius's heart!

Let's Play!

Unscramble the missing words to review today's part of Cornelius's story.

Cornelius was Roman _____, which meant
IONCENRUT
he was a soldier in charge of about 100 other soldiers.

Cornelius _____ in God.
EIEEBLVD

Cornelius often showed _____ to the Jewish people in Caesarea. SKSIENDN

An angel told Cornelius to send to _____ for a man named _____. PPOJA
REPTE

 **PRAY**

Thank God that He looks at the heart! Ask Him to make your heart look more like His.

79

Meanwhile Peter . . .

Again, a second time, the voice said to him,
"What God has made clean, do not
call impure."—Acts 10:15

In the previous devotion, you read about Cornelius who was in Caesarea. Meanwhile, Peter was staying at someone's house in Joppa. Peter went up on the patio-like rooftop to wait for the meal to be prepared and to pray. Peter also saw a vision from God. He saw what looked like a sheet being lowered from heaven. All sorts of unclean animals were in it. Jewish law said they could not eat them. Before Jesus died on the cross, God told His people to avoid certain foods because they made them unclean, or unable to go before God. This was called a "ceremonial law."

However, after Jesus died on the cross, people no longer had to worry about that kind of law. A voice told Peter to prepare and eat from the selection. Peter said, "No. I've never eaten anything that was unclean!" The voice told Peter not to call something unclean if God has made it clean. Peter saw the whole vision and heard the words three times. God was reminding Peter that Jesus ultimately made him clean by dying on the cross.

Let's Play!

Across

4. Where was Cornelius?
6. Who went up on the roof to pray?
7. Peter thought the animals were _____.

Down

1. When Peter was on the roof, he saw a _____.
2. How many times did Peter see the vision?
3. Where was Peter?
4. What was the name of the Roman Centurion?
5. What was in the sheet that Peter saw?

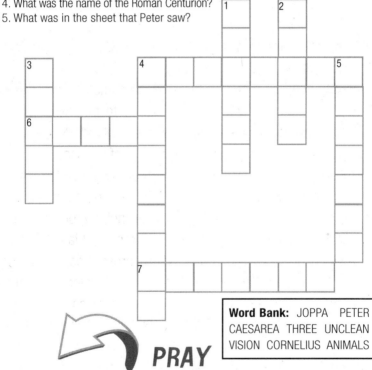

Word Bank: JOPPA   PETER   CAESAREA   THREE   UNCLEAN   VISION   CORNELIUS   ANIMALS

PRAY

Thank God that Jesus died to make you clean so you can have a relationship with God.

80

The Gospel Is for Everyone

Peter began to speak: "Now I truly understand that God doesn't show favoritism."—Acts 10:34

Let's recap the first two parts of our story. An angel told Cornelius, a centurion who loved God, to send for a man named Peter in Joppa. Meanwhile, Peter had a vision about things he thought were unclean, but God said they were now clean. Just as Peter's vision ended, the three men Cornelius sent knocked at the door. God is always in control—His timing is amazing! Peter went with the men back to Caesarea. When they got there, Cornelius told Peter about his vision four days earlier. Peter entered Cornelius's house and discovered a large crowd of people that Cornelius had gathered to hear Peter's message.

Peter realized his vision meant that the gospel was for all people whether they were Jewish or not, and he began to preach about Jesus. Before Peter could finish, the Holy Spirit filled those who were listening, and they became believers, too! Peter led the group to be baptized as new followers of Jesus.

Level Up!

We read about three parts of this amazing story during three devotional times. You can read the whole story for yourself in your Bible (Acts 10:1–48).

List any facts you discovered when you read the Scripture that was not included in the devotions.

PRAY

Thank God that His plan is to save people from everywhere. Thank Him that the gospel is for everyone—even you!

81
Proof

When they heard this they became silent.
And they glorified God, saying, "So then,
God has given repentance resulting in
life even to the Gentiles."—Acts 11:18

Mr. Lopez finished telling the Bible story about Peter and Cornelius to his Sunday morning Bible study group. Ivan had been listening carefully to the story but quickly asked, "Were the other believers excited to hear about the new believers in Caesarea?"

"You would think so," Mr. Lopez explained. "But remember, they still thought that Jesus came to be the Savior of the Jewish people only. They didn't realize Jesus came as the Savior of the world. Peter helped them understand how God proved Jesus was for everyone. First, Peter told them about his vision and what it meant. Then, Peter told them how the Holy Spirit had filled those at Cornelius's house when they believed. God gave proof that salvation can be for anyone."

"Were the believers in Jerusalem excited after they heard Peter's evidence?" Ivan asked.

"They were," Mr. Lopez agreed. "The Bible says they glorified God."

Challenge Accepted!

Peter told his friends in Jerusalem how he knew Cornelius and his family were believers in Jesus.

How can people know you are a Christian?

What evidence helps you know someone else is a Christian?

 **PRAY**

Thank God for new believers who have recently trusted in Jesus as Savior.

82

Wake-Up Call

*Motioning to them with his hand to be silent,
he [Peter] described to them how the Lord had
brought him out of the prison.—Acts 12:17*

Ameres's mom flipped on the light in his bedroom. He groaned and rolled over. Mom shook his foot and said, "Get up, sleepyhead, we're leaving for Grandpa's today, and we want to get on the road early." Ameres sat up, rubbing his eyes. "Get dressed and grab your backpack. It's a good thing you got it ready last night!"

Later, when they were in the car, they were talking about how Ameres had a hard time getting up and moving that morning. "You remind me of Peter from the story in our family Bible study," Mom said.

Ameres laughed, "That's one of my favorites. It was sad that Peter was in prison, but it was amazing how God rescued him. The angel had a hard time getting Peter up and moving, too."

"That's right," Mom agreed. "Even the people gathered at Mary's house to pray were surprised when their prayer was answered."

Level Up!

Ameres said this story is one of his favorites. Make your way through the maze, then check out the story for yourself!

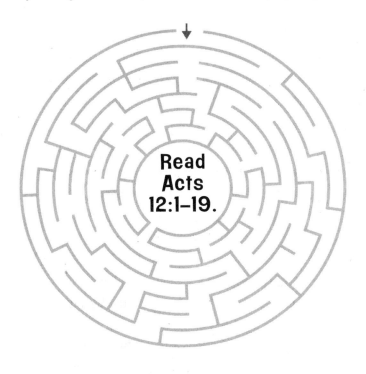

Read Acts 12:1–19.

 **PRAY**

Talk to God about some of your favorite parts in the Bible. Thank Him for how they help you.

83

Peter, the Letter Writer

Blessed be the God and Father of our Lord Jesus Christ. Because of his great mercy he has given us new birth into a living hope through the resurrection of Jesus Christ from the dead.—1 Peter 1:3

In New Testament times, early church leaders wrote letters to groups of believers who lived far away. These letters were passed around from church to church to help and encourage the believers. Two of Peter's letters are part of our New Testament. Peter wrote the first of his two letters to believers who left their homes and moved far away. Peter wanted to encourage the new believers to remember to put their faith in God, even if the people in the new place they lived didn't worship God.

Peter reminded them that our permanent home isn't on this earth, but a new earth that Jesus will create when He comes back. In that earth, there will be no more difficulties, hard times, or suffering. Peter knew the people were facing tough times. He reminded them that Jesus's resurrection from the dead gives true hope. The hope we have in Jesus is not a maybe kind of hope, but a for-sure kind of hope.

Trivia Time!

Check out these facts about Peter, the writer. Circle what you didn't know before!

- Peter's first letter went to believers living in what is now Turkey.

- First Peter was probably written sometime between AD 62 and 64.

- Nero was Emperor of Rome during the time Peter wrote his letters.

- Peter was probably in Rome when he wrote the letters.

PRAY

Thank God that we know Jesus will do the things He promises. He will return someday.

84

Be Holy

But as the one who called you is holy, you also are to be holy in your conduct; for it is written, Be holy, because I am holy.—1 Peter 1:15–16

Mimi, what does it mean to be holy like God is holy? I'm not God," Josie asked her grandmother.

Mimi smiled. She understood Josie's confusion because she had been confused by that Bible verse for a long time, too. She explained: "Holy means set apart. God is perfect and set apart from all of His creation. He cannot sin. And He wants us to live that way, too. Even though we will never be perfect in this life, if we believe in Jesus, God sets us apart. We are different from the world because we have been saved by Jesus, and we are called to live in a way that shows that. We should try to live set-apart lives by honoring God."

"Wow," Josie said, pondering what Mimi had told her. "What if we mess up?"

Mimi assured her, "The good news is, God has set us apart in Jesus, and we can't mess that up! Even when we fail to be holy, we are still set apart in Christ, and we have new chances every day to live in a way that represents that."

Challenge Accepted!

Growing as a Christian means spending time doing things that help you focus more on God. Rate each of the following spiritual disciplines on the graph, then think of one thing you can do to improve that habit in your life.

Reading my Bible

| Never | Almost Never | Sometimes | Often | Very Often |

Praying

| Never | Almost Never | Sometimes | Often | Very Often |

Bible study and worship with other believers

| Never | Almost Never | Sometimes | Often | Very Often |

 **PRAY**

Ask God to help you honor Him.

85

Honor Everyone

Honor everyone. Love the brothers and sisters. Fear God. Honor the emperor.—1 Peter 2:17

Walker dropped his backpack on the kitchen table with a thud. Today had not been a good day. Mom put some groceries in the refrigerator, then turned to Walker, "Your teacher sent me an email this afternoon. She said you refused to follow one of her rules today. She said it's a warning, but if you get another bad mark, you won't get to go on the field trip. Can you help me understand what happened?"

"Mrs. Jones has dumb rules!" Walker exclaimed. "I was tired of doing math. I decided to work on my science instead. Why should it matter if I'm doing something?"

"Do you remember the Bible verse we read last night about honoring everyone?" Mom asked. "Peter wrote to people who were being mistreated by the emperor. Peter explained that Christians should show respect and honor even when they disagree with a rule. I think you need to apologize to Mrs. Jones tomorrow and do your math during math time."

Let's Play!

Can you find these words in the word search? How does each word remind you of a truth from today's devotion?

Word Bank: RULES OBEY HONOR RESPECT
LEADERS LOVE PETER AUTHORITY

```
F  L  K  H  A  I  J  M  N  Y
X  E  P  K  U  I  W  J  J  O
L  A  E  N  T  J  C  C  N  D
W  D  T  J  H  O  N  O  R  R
L  E  E  R  O  T  K  S  K  E
O  R  R  O  R  R  U  L  E  S
L  S  P  S  I  O  U  H  X  P
H  O  B  O  T  B  B  B  D  E
T  X  V  P  Y  D  L  E  I  C
E  M  U  E  U  Y  G  I  Y  T
```

 **PRAY**

*Ask God to help you be respectful even
when you disagree with the rules.*

86
Tell What You Know

But in your hearts regard Christ the Lord as holy, ready at any time to give a defense to anyone who asks you for a reason for the hope that is in you.—1 Peter 3:15

Amaya found her dad working at his desk. "Dad, may I ask you a question?"

Dad finished typing his email and then turned to Amaya, "Sure. What's going on?"

"I have a friend at school who told me she didn't believe the Bible, and she thought Jesus was just someone who told good stories and did good things. I don't like to argue with her, but I really believe the Bible is true and Jesus is God."

"I'm glad you don't want to argue, but it's ok to disagree if you are kind and respectful. First, you need to know what you believe and why. Reading your Bible and studying it with your Bible study groups helps you know and remember what the Bible says. Then, don't be afraid to kindly say what you believe," Dad encouraged her. "And let's pray that God will help your friend know He loves her."

Challenge Accepted!

Reading your Bible and listening to your church teachers and pastor can help you know what you believe. Usually, the best thing you can do is simply tell people who Jesus is and what He came to do.

Can you describe how you became a Christian and trusted Jesus as your Savior?

Can you think of times God showed His love and care for you?

 **PRAY**

Ask God to help you know what to say when you talk to friends who don't believe in Jesus.

87

A Happy Heart

*Be hospitable to one another without
complaining.—1 Peter 4:9*

Have you ever had a chore to do that you didn't like?
Maybe it was taking out the trash or helping carry groceries. Were you happy to do it, or did you grumble? In New
Testament times, people would stop at a home and ask
for a place to spend the night back then while they were
traveling. In his letter, Peter told the people to "be hospitable," or care for one another without complaining. Attitude
affects everything we do. If we grumble and complain, it is
unpleasant for the people we're supposed to be helping,
and it takes *our* joy away. We can't feel joy when we are
complaining.

The Bible tells us to do everything as if we are doing it
for Jesus. The Bible also says to "serve the LORD with gladness" (Psalm 100:2). When you want to give God glory,
you naturally help others with a better attitude and a more
hospitable heart.

Level Up!

Read a little more of Peter's instructions in this letter he sent to believers. What are some other truths in these verses? Write them in the bubbles!

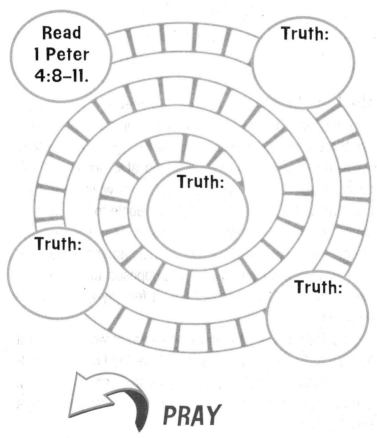

Read
1 Peter
4:8–11.

Truth:

Truth:

Truth:

Truth:

PRAY

*Ask God to help you remember to honor
Him on days you feel grumpy.*

88

In Tough Times

If you are ridiculed for the name of Christ,
you are blessed, because the Spirit of glory
and of God rests on you.—1 Peter 4:14

It hurts when people tease us or make fun of us, especially if they make fun of us for personal things like our family, our friends, or our beliefs. Have you ever been made fun of because you go to church or talk about God? It is important to remember a few things. First, the people who make fun of us probably don't know Jesus. They don't have the Holy Spirit in their hearts helping them understand the truth, so going to church and talking about God may be genuinely confusing to them.

That doesn't make teasing okay, but it may help us understand why it happens. Second, in his letter, Peter said that God blesses us when we experience mistreatment for belief in Jesus. God is honored when we are faithful to Him and to His Son. The important thing to remember is that God has given us the Holy Spirit who is with us and strengthens us, especially in tough times.

Challenge Accepted!

How do you know God helps you even if others put you down? Read Isaiah 41:10 and then list how God helps you.

 **PRAY**

Ask God to help you honor Him even if those around you make fun of your beliefs.

89

God Cares

Casting all your cares on him, because he cares about you.—1 Peter 5:7

Lukas was spending the weekend with his grandparents. One morning, he came to breakfast and saw his Papa reading his Bible. "You read your Bible a lot, don't you, Papa?" Lukas asked.

"I do. The older I get, the more I realize how much I need it. I wish I had started reading it when I was younger," Papa said.

"I like reading parts of the Bible. Some parts are hard to understand," Lukas admitted.

"Some parts are still hard for me," Papa said. "But there are so many passages in the Bible that are so encouraging to me. When I struggle to understand one part, I try to rely on the parts I do understand. For example, the Bible tells us God cares about us, so we can give all our concerns to Him. He will help us no matter what. Let's start making a list of some concerns we can pray to God about."

"Great idea, Papa!" Lukas agreed.

Let's Play!

Solve the code to discover the Bible book names, then locate each verse in your Bible. How can each verse help you when you are afraid, angry, fearful, or worried?

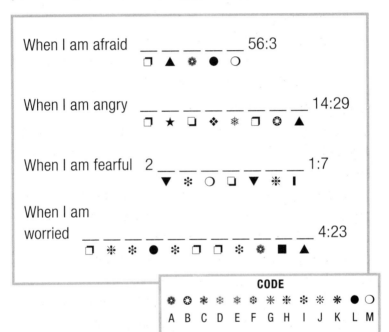

When I am afraid _ _ _ _ _ 56:3
◻ ▲ ❀ ● ○

When I am angry _ _ _ _ _ _ _ _ 14:29
◻ ★ ❑ ❖ ❊ ◻ ◉ ▲

When I am fearful 2 _ _ _ _ _ _ _ 1:7
▼ ❊ ○ ❑ ▼ ❊ ❙

When I am worried _ _ _ _ _ _ _ _ _ ■ ▲ 4:23
◻ ❊ ❊ ● ❊ ◻ ◻ ❊ ❀ ■ ▲

CODE

❀	◉	❋	❊	❊	❊	❊	❊	❊	❊	❊	●	○
A	B	C	D	E	F	G	H	I	J	K	L	M

■	❑	◻	❑	★	▲	▼	◆	❖	❙	❙	❙	❙
N	O	P	Q	R	S	T	U	V	W	X	Y	Z

PRAY

Thank God for all the places in the Bible that help you know how much He cares for you.

90

Everything We Need

His divine power has given us everything required for life and godliness.—2 Peter 1:3

Peter wrote letters to encourage and help believers. In Peter's second letter, he encouraged believers to grow in their faith. That means Peter told them to keep praying and learning from the Scriptures. Peter knew that no one can live a perfect life honoring God without God's help. Do you remember how Peter once turned his back on Jesus by denying Him, but Jesus loved and forgave him?

Peter wrote about the power God gives us that helps us live lives that give honor to God. Peter said God's power gives us *everything* we need to live lives pleasing to God. The "life" Peter was talking about is eternal life. God's power helps us live in our world here and now. God's power will also be with us for life eternal when believers join Jesus in heaven.

Challenge Accepted!

Remember these definitions:

> **Life = Eternal Life**

> **Godliness = godly or God-pleasing living**

Why do you think we need God's divine power for eternal life and godly living?

 **PRAY**

Thank God that when you feel like you're messing up or disappointing Him, He promises to help you. Ask God to give you the power to honor Him.

91
Precious Promises

By these he has given us very great and precious promises, so that through them you may share in the divine nature, escaping the corruption that is in the world because of evil desire.—2 Peter 1:4

Isabel's mom helped her pack her things for the sleepover at Kehlani's house. Kehlani was Isabel's new friend. "Are you excited about the sleepover?" Mom asked. "I talked to Kehlani's mom before we agreed to let you go, and I know her parents will be home and supervising. It sounds like there are six of you going."

Isabel nodded happily. "We all spend recess at school together. Most of us are in the same classes." Then Isabel looked serious. "I do want to make good choices, but I know some of the other girls do some things I am not allowed to do. They are really nice! I just feel differently about some things than them."

Mom nodded. "Let's pray together right now that God will help you be a great friend, but also have the courage to make choices you know will please God."

Level Up!

Peter wrote about God's "precious promises" that help us live godly lives. Look up these precious promises. Make a check mark by each one after you read it. Write your favorite promise in the box below.

- ☐ Joshua 1:9
- ☐ Psalm 32:8
- ☐ Ephesians 2:10
- ☐ Hebrews 10:23
- ☐ James 1:5

 **PRAY**

*Ask God to help you have the courage to make
the right choices even when you're tempted
to do things that won't please Him.*

92

Eyewitnesses

*For he received honor and glory from
God the Father when the voice came to him
from the Majestic Glory, saying "This is
my beloved Son, with whom I am
well-pleased!"—2 Peter 1:17*

Peter knew many people would listen when his letters were read. He told his listeners that the events he described were not made-up stories. They were real! Peter and the other disciples were there and saw many things that took place while Jesus was on earth. Peter described the majesty of Jesus. He wrote about hearing the voice of God the Father saying, "This is my beloved Son, with whom I am well pleased!"

How do you feel when you hear a person describe something they saw with their own eyes? When they talk about it, does it seem more real to you? Peter was trying to help his readers know the things he said happened were true. He wanted the original listeners and those of us who read his words to be certain that Jesus came to earth and that God the Father declared Jesus is His Son.

Let's Play!

Across

3. God said about Jesus, "This is My _____ Son."
4. 1 Peter and 2 Peter were first written as _____.
6. Peter described events in the life of _____.
7. God said He was well- _____ with Jesus.

Down

1. Peter and the disciples saw things first-hand. They were _____.
2. Who wrote 1 Peter and 2 Peter?
5. Peter said the events he described were not made-up stories, they were _____.

Word Bank: PLEASED PETER EYEWITNESSES BELOVED JESUS LETTERS REAL

PRAY

Thank God for the many ways He proves who Jesus is. Ask God to help you grow in your belief.

93

God's Word Is from God

Because no prophecy ever came by the will of man; instead, men spoke from God as they were carried along by the Holy Spirit.—2 Peter 1:21

When Peter wrote his letters, he didn't know they would become part of our Bible. At that time, the only Scripture was the Old Testament. God's plan was for the prophets to write about Jesus coming and the New Testament writers to write about the things Jesus did and why He came.

Peter told his readers that no Scripture came about because the prophet (or writer) was making it. Instead, God guided exactly what was written through the power of the Holy Spirit.

God used many different writers over the course of centuries to write down the truths we have in our Bibles. The writers lived in many different places, at many different times, and in many different circumstances; however, when you read the Bible, you will discover it all works together to help us know God's story.

Trivia Time!

How many of these Bible trivia facts did you know?

☐ 66: There are 66 books in the Bible.

☐ 2: There are 2 Testaments (Old and New).

☐ 39: There are 39 books in the Old Testament.

☐ 27: There are 27 books in the New Testament.

☐ 35+: The Bible was written by more than 35 writers.

☐ 1: The 1 true source of the Bible is God.

☐ 400: About 400 years passed between the last book of the Old Testament and the first book of the New Testament.

 **PRAY**

Thank God for the amazing way He gave us His Word. Thank Him for your Bible.

94

Jesus Is Coming Back

The Lord does not delay his promise, as some understand delay, but is patient with you, not wanting any to perish but all to come to repentance.—2 Peter 3:9

Jaden and his dad walked to the car after church. "The pastor was really excited talking about Jesus's return, wasn't he?" Jaden asked.

"He was," Dad agreed. "And it is exciting to think about. Jesus has always kept His promises. So, when He said He is coming back, you can be sure He will!"

"But when, Dad?" Jaden asked. "I've heard people talk about signs. Do you think we will know when He's coming?"

Dad replied. "Jesus told His followers that only God the Father knows when Jesus's return will be, so it really isn't helpful to try and figure it out. The Bible also says that God's timing is not like ours. And we know that while we wait, God wants us to tell others about Jesus so they can believe in Him, too."

Challenge Accepted!

How do you feel when you think about Jesus returning?

If you knew He was coming back tomorrow, what would you do today?

Why is Jesus's coming back going to be such a great thing?

PRAY

Talk to Jesus about how you feel about His returning.
Thank Him for keeping His promises.

95

Final Words

But grow in the grace and knowledge of our Lord and Savior Jesus Christ. To him be the glory both now and to the day of eternity.—2 Peter 3:18

Today's Bible verse is the last verse of the last letter Peter wrote. You've done an amazing job as we've looked at verses that told us about Peter, about his experiences with Jesus, and about how Jesus prepared Peter to be an important leader. God used Peter in big ways, but Peter was simply a man who followed God. Peter told his readers to continue to grow "in the grace and knowledge of our Lord and Savior Jesus Christ."

Becoming a Christian isn't only something to do. It means becoming a follower of Jesus Christ. As you pray and read your Bible, you get to know Jesus better. You begin to realize how much He helps you each day. The study of Peter's life helps us realize that God loves us even when we mess up. God had a plan for Peter, and He has a plan for you. The last few devotions will help you think about ways to keep studying God's Word. Like Peter, the more you know about God, the more you can give Jesus glory for the rest of your life.

Let's Play!

Find these words in the word search. How do all these words help you remember facts about Peter?

Word Bank: FISHERMAN DISCIPLE LEADER PREACHER
WRITER FOLLOWER BELIEVER FORGIVEN

B	W	R	I	T	E	R	F	C	N
E	F	G	P	L	E	H	I	W	F
L	O	B	R	O	C	C	S	O	F
I	L	Z	E	J	D	K	H	I	O
E	L	E	A	D	E	R	E	T	R
V	O	B	C	H	R	M	R	O	G
E	W	S	H	Z	D	R	M	R	I
R	E	L	E	U	L	Z	A	Z	V
J	R	A	R	V	L	W	N	C	E
D	I	S	C	I	P	L	E	V	N

 **PRAY**

*Thank God for believers like Peter, whose examples
help you know how to be a follower of Jesus.*

96

Memorizing Scripture

You have revealed the paths of life to me; you will fill me with gladness in your presence.—Acts 2:28

What are you doing?" Georgia asked her big sister, June. June was writing on a sticky note and putting it on her mirror.

"I'm trying to memorize Bible verses, so I thought if I wrote the verse on sticky notes and put them wherever I look throughout the day, it might help me," June explained.

"You better put one on your phone then," Georgia teased her sister.

June showed Georgia her phone. The verse was her screen saver. "Already thought of that!" June replied. "You can help me practice. Look at the words on my phone while I say the verse." June quoted Acts 2:28 without missing a word.

"Great job!" Georgia said.

"It's a verse from Peter's sermon in Acts, but he was actually quoting a psalm," June explained. "It's fun to know about a verse when you memorize it."

Challenge Accepted!

Have you ever compared a verse in the New Testament that quotes a verse in the Old Testament? Sometimes the words are slightly different because the originals of both were written in different languages, but the truth is clearly the same.

Compare these two Scriptures:

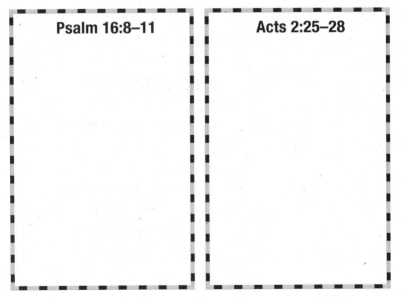

Psalm 16:8–11	Acts 2:25–28

 **PRAY**

Ask God to help you discover
Bible verses you can memorize.

97

Pondering Scripture

He renews my life; he leads me
along the right paths for his
name's sake.—Psalm 23:3

Memorizing Scripture is a great way to "grow in grace" as Peter's letter encouraged his readers to do. Another way to focus on Scripture is to ponder or meditate. Both words mean to "think hard" or "focus" on something. You could choose a verse or a passage to read each morning and think about it off and on throughout the day. Copy the words in a journal. Ponder the same verse or passage for a week or longer. Write down what that verse helps you know.

Choosing a verse or passage to read right before you go to bed is a great idea, too. Think or ponder about the words you read as you drift off to sleep. Sometimes the things we see or experience throughout the day can be troubling. Focusing on God's Word before going to sleep can help our minds stay on Him rather than the things that trouble us.

Level Up!

If you don't have a Bible passage picked out already, locate Psalm 23.

- Copy a few verses in your journal or a notebook.

- Read it every day for a week or even a month.

- Each day add a note about something you discover as you read the psalm. Is there something you understand better or maybe something you want to ask a Christian adult about?

- Pray before you read the psalm each day and ask God to help you grow to know Him better.

PRAY

Thank God for His Word that teaches us, comforts us, and guides us.

98

Studying Scripture

Trust in the LORD with all your heart, and do not rely on your own understanding; in all your ways know him, and he will make your paths straight.—Proverbs 3:5–6

A proverb is a wise saying. It is usually short and gives good advice. King Solomon was known for his God-given wisdom and is the writer of most of the book of Proverbs in the Bible. Today's verse is a reminder to trust in the Lord rather than in your own wisdom or what you think. The promise in the verse says that if you focus on God, He will direct your path.

Studying Scripture means learning about it as well as memorizing it. It helps to learn things about a verse like who wrote it, what else did he write, or how did God use him during his lifetime. It means trusting that God is always in control, and His way is *always* best! How do you find out that kind of information? Many study Bibles have notes at the beginning of each Bible book or near sections of verses. There are even study Bibles for kids and teens! Some Bibles are made so you can write notes in the margin, or some people like to keep a Bible study notebook handy. What's your favorite way to remember what you read?

Trivia Time!

What tools can you use to study the Bible? Here are a few:

Bible Dictionary: definitions about words unique to the Bible or information about items and places in the Bible

Bible Atlas: maps and charts to discover things like distances between places or sites of biblical locations

Commentaries: books of study notes created by biblical scholars that help give background information about a verse or passage

Concordance: lists of Bible verses based on keywords or topics

Bible apps: the Bible in a variety of translations (versions) and tools like the ones already listed but in digital form

 **PRAY**

Thank God for the ways He has given you to study His Word. Thank Him for the Holy Spirit who helps us as we read the Bible.

99

Obeying Scripture

The one who follows instruction is on the path to life, but the one who rejects correction goes astray.—Proverbs 10:17

Zayn was helping his big brother, Derek, get ready to mow the yard. Zayn propped the weed eater against the garage and asked, "Are there rules everywhere about everything you do?"

Derek looked surprised. "I guess about most things. Why?"

Zayn shrugged and said, "We got our science kits at school, but we had to have an hour of safety class first. Then we learned a new game in P.E. class, but we had to go over the rules first."

"Oh, I see what you mean," Derek replied as he carefully poured gas in the mower. "I remember when Dad taught me the rules about how to take care of the mower. But that's so we stay safe when we use it. I guess most rules help everyone know what to do so they can enjoy things and not get hurt."

Let's Play!

Can you find these words from Proverbs 10:17?

Word Bank: CORRECTION PROVERBS FOLLOWS
REJECTS ASTRAY PATH LIFE ONE

A	T	R	C	Y	N	S	D	Y	P
Q	S	T	O	L	I	F	E	S	R
L	F	T	R	Q	J	O	N	E	O
I	O	Z	R	E	M	J	P	W	V
P	L	C	E	A	J	E	I	O	E
E	L	K	C	R	Y	E	U	B	R
P	O	R	T	G	Z	T	C	E	B
A	W	U	I	I	I	S	X	T	S
T	S	Y	O	Q	O	L	L	F	S
H	P	T	N	A	S	B	P	H	Y

PRAY

Thank God for His instructions in the Bible. Thank Him for providing them so we can live a life that honors Him.

100
Treasuring Scripture

I have treasured your word in my heart so that I may not sin against you.—Psalm 119:11

What do you treasure? When you treasure something, it means it is important to you. You can treasure a memory, like a special trip you took. You can treasure a gift, like a quilt your grandma made. Most of us treasure the people in our family and our close friends. The psalmist said in Psalm 119 that he treasured God's Word because when God's Word was important to him, it helped him resist the temptation to sin.

When he experienced twists and turns, the Bible helped guide his path. You can choose a lot of things to fill your mind and your time with. Many are fun. Some are good for your body and your mind. Taking time every day to focus on God is one of the best choices you can make. Now that you have finished this book, think about what you will do next to treasure God's Word so you will trust Him through every twist and turn!

Challenge Accepted!

What will you challenge yourself to do to keep growing spiritually?

What book of the Bible will you read next?

When is your best prayer time?

Where do you go to worship God with other believers?

 **PRAY**

Thank God for helping you grow to become the person He created you to be. Praise Him that through life's twists and turns, He is always in control and His way is always best.

Answers to Activities

PAGE 7

PAGE 11

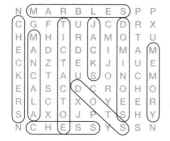

PAGE 27

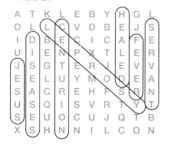

PAGE 47

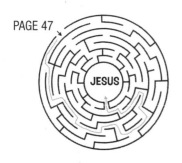

PAGE 57

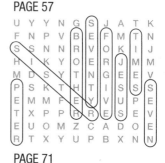

PAGE 71

PAGE 77

PAGE 89

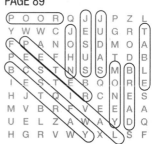

PAGE 105

Crossword answers:
- 1 Down: COURTYARD
- 2 Across: JOHN
- 3 Down: NIGHTPRIEST (N-I-G-H-T-P-R-I-E-S-T)
- 4 Across: PETER
- 5 Across: GATEKEEPER
- 6 Across: JESUS

PAGE 141

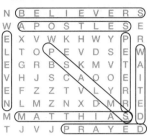

Word search grid:
```
N B E L I E V E R S
W A P O S T L E S E
E X V W K H W Y P R
L T O P E V D S E W
E G R B S K M V T A
V H J S C A O O E I
E F Z Z T V L Y R T
N L M Z N X D M R E
M M A T T H I A S D
T J V J P R A Y E D
```
Words: BELIEVERS, APOSTLES, WAITED, MATTHIAS, PRAYED

PAGE 113

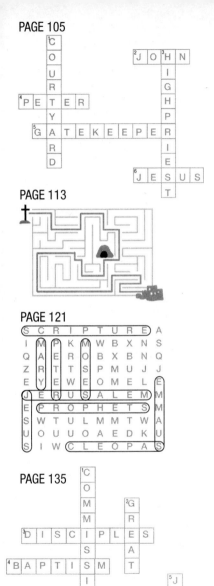

PAGE 163

Crossword answers:
- 1 Down: VISION
- 2 Down: THE
- 3 Down: JOPPA
- 4 Across: CAESAREA
- 5 Down: ANIMALS
- 6 Across: PETER
- 7 Across: UNCLEAN
- Down (under 4): CORNELIUS

PAGE 121

Word search grid:
```
S C R I P T U R E A
I M P K M W B X N S
Q A E R O B X B N Q
Z R T T S P M U J J
E Y E W E O M E L E
J E R U S A L E M M
E P R O P H E T S M
S W T U L M M T W A
U O U U O A E D K U
S I W C L E O P A S
```
Words: SCRIPTURE, JERUSALEM, PROPHETS, CLEOPAS

PAGE 135

Crossword answers:
- 1 Down: COMMANDS (C-O-M-M-A...)
- 2 Down: GREAT
- 3 Across: DISCIPLES
- 4 Across: BAPTISM
- 5 Down: JESUS
- 6 Across: NATIONS

PAGE 169

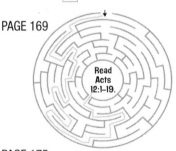

Read Acts 12:1–19.

PAGE 175

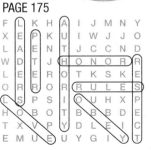

Word search grid:
```
F L K H A I J M N Y
X E P K U I W J J O
L A E N T J C C N D
W D T J H O N O R R
L E E R O T K S K E
O R R O R R U L E S
L S P S I O U H X P
H O B O T B B B B D
T X V P Y D L E I C
E M U E U Y G I Y T
```
Words: LEADERS, AUTHORITY, HONOR, RULES, RESPECT

207

PAGE 189

PAGE 195

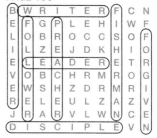

PAGE 203

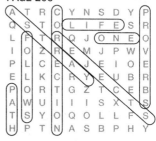

PAGE 33
SIMON PETER, JAMES, JOHN, ANDREW, PHILIP, BARTHOLOMEW, MATTHEW, THOMAS, JAMES, ALPHAEUS, THADDAEUS, SIMON, JUDAS ISCARIOT

PAGE 35
THE DISCIPLES, TWELVE, PETER

PAGE 45
DISCIPLES, JESUS, PETER, MESSIAH, FATHER IN HEAVEN

PAGE 51
NETS, HOOK, FIRST, COIN, JESUS, PETER

PAGE 91
BETRAY, DENY, LOVE, ROOSTER, JESUS

PAGE 99
FORGIVENESS, WISDOM, RIGHT THING, COURAGE, MAKE THINGS RIGHT

PAGE 117
EMPTY, RACED, JOHN, PETER

PAGE 161
CENTURION, BELIEVED, KINDNESS, JOPPA, PETER

PAGE 183
PSALM, PROVERBS, TIMOTHY, PHILIPPIANS